WORLD'S BEST RECIPES

From 100 Countries and Regions

Recipes excerpted from
50 Hippocrene International Cookbooks

Compiled by
the Editors of Hippocrene Books

HIPPOCRENE BOOKS
New York

For information, address:
HIPPOCRENE BOOKS, INC.
171 Madison Avenue
New York, NY 10016

Cataloging-in-Publication data available from the Library of Congress.

ISBN 0-7818-0599-6

Printed in the United States of America.

Table of Contents

Vegetables   83

Fish & Seafood 181

Appetizers &
Side Dishes

Basic Cheese Fondue

Ingredients

1 pound Switzerland Swiss cheese or
　　half Emmertaler and half Gruyère, shredded
　　or diced; or the equivalent in slices finely cut
3 tablespoons all-purpose flour, or
　　1½ tablespoons cornstarch
1 garlic clove
2 cups dry white wine such as Fleuchâtel or any light dry
　　wine of the Rhine (Riesling) or Chablis type
1 tablespoon lemon juice
3 tablespoons Kirsch or brandy
Nutmeg, pepper or paprika, to taste
2 loaves Italian or French bread, cut in cubes, crust on
　　each side

Dredge the cheese lightly with the flour. Rub the cooking pot with garlic; pour in the wine; set over moderate heat. When air bubbles rise to surface, add lemon juice. Then add the cheese by handfuls, stirring constantly with a wooden fork or spoon until the cheese is melting. Add the Kirsch and spices, stirring until blended. Serve and keep bubbling hot over burner. Spear the bread cubes through the soft side into the crust, dunk and swirl in the fondue.

Makes 4 servings

From: *The Swiss Cookbook*

 Basic Corn Tortillas

This basic recipe is very quick and easy to make from either fresh *masa* or *masa harina*. Strange as it may seem, the substitution of *masa harina* and water does not result in an exact substitution of measurements. Two cups of fresh *masa* equals 2 cups of *masa harina* and 1 cup of water.

Ingredients

2 cups fresh *masa*, or 2 cups *masa harina* and
    1 cup water

Have also on hand
Tortilla press
2 plastic baggies or pieces of wax paper to sandwich
    the ball
Griddle or heavy skillet
Basket or bowl lined with napkin or towel

For Fresh Masa:
Fresh *masa* needs no preparation or additional ingredients. Keep it moist by covering it with a damp towel.

For Masa Harina:
Mix the *masa harina* and water thoroughly.

For both Masa *and* Masa Harina:
Have the tortilla press, baggies/wax paper, griddle or heavy skillet, and cloth-lined basket ready. Heat the heavy skillet or griddle until a drop of water bounces from it. Form a walnut-sized ball of dough from either the *masa* or *masa harina*. Place 1 baggie or piece of wax paper on the bottom section of the press. Place a ball of dough on the press just slightly above the center and

3

top it with the second baggie. Press the handle down firmly on the press, peel off the plastic or wax paper and place the tortilla on the griddle. Toast for about 1½ minutes, flip and toast for about 45 seconds more. Flip the third time, pressing on the tortilla with fingers or spatula to encourage the bread to inflate. Cook on third side only about 30 seconds. Do not overcook—tortillas dry out easily. Place each tortilla in a cloth-lined basket to keep it warm and continue to cook the remaining breads.

Makes about 16 (4-inch) tortillas

From: **Mayan Cooking: Recipes from the Sun Kingdoms of Mexico**
(Guatemala)

 **Kulikuli**

Ingredients

2 cups shelled roasted peanuts, unsalted
Salt
Peanut oil

Grind the nuts very fine. Place in a clean dish towel and squeeze out as much oil as possible. Mix the nuts with salt to taste and enough warm water to make a stiff but pliable dough. Form into balls, rings, or any shape desired and fry in hot oil until golden-brown.

Makes about 46 (1-inch) balls

From: **Best of Regional African Cooking**
(Nigeria)

4

Armenian Meat Pies
Missahatz or Lahmajoon

for the Dough
¾ cup warm water
(110 to 115 degrees)
1 package active dry yeast
2¼ cups sifted all-purpose flour
½ teaspoon salt
½ teaspoon sugar
¼ cup melted butter or margarine

for the Meat Topping
1 pound lean ground lamb
1 medium onion, finely chopped
¼ cup finely chopped green pepper
1 medium ripe tomato, peeled, seeded, and finely
    chopped
¼ cup parsley, finely chopped
1 tablespoon fresh mint leaves, finely chopped
2 tablespoons tomato paste
3 tablespoons lemon juice, freshly squeezed and
    strained
½ teaspoon allspice, or ¼ teaspoon each allspice
    and cinnamon
Freshly ground black pepper, salt
Middle East red pepper
Paprika

To make the dough, pour ½ cup of the water into a small
bowl and add the yeast. Let stand 3 minutes, then stir to dissolve
yeast completely.

5

In a deep bowl combine the flour, salt, and sugar. Make a well in the center and pour in the yeast mixture, melted butter, and remaining ¼ cup water. Using a large spoon, gradually blend the liquids into the flour mixture, working from the center out. Beat until the ingredients are well-blended and form a soft dough.

Place the dough on a lightly floured surface and knead thoroughly, sprinkling occasionally with just enough flour to keep it from sticking. When it is smooth and elastic in texture, form into a lump and place in a lightly oiled bowl. Cover loosely with a kitchen towel and leave to rise in a warm place 2 to 3 hours or until doubled in size.

Meanwhile, combine all the topping ingredients except the paprika in a deep bowl and knead well until thoroughly blended. Cover and refrigerate.

Punch down the dough and divide into 12 equal pieces. Form each into a ball and place on a lightly floured surface. Cover with a cloth and let rest 15 minutes.

On a lightly floured surface roll out each of the balls into a circle approximately 6 inches in diameter. Place ⅓ to ½ cup topping in the center of each circle, then spread it evenly to within about ¼ inch of the edge.

Arrange the pies on lightly oiled baking sheets. Bake in a preheated 450 degree oven about 12 minutes or until lightly browned. You may place the pies briefly under the broiler to brown the tops. Sprinkle with paprika and serve hot or at room temperature, accompanied by lemon wedges or plain yogurt, if desired.

TIPS:
For quick and easy lahmajoon, substitute pita breads, halved horizontally to form rounds, or flour tortillas for the dough.

Makes 12 servings

From: *Cuisine of Armenia*

Wedding Pilaf
Harsanik Yeghintz

The color, romance, and splendor of the East are expressed in this magnificent and opulent pilaf, which Caucasian Armenians reserve for great occasions.

Ingredients

2 tablespoons butter
⅓ cup dried apricots
⅓ cup dried prunes, pitted
⅓ cup dried currants
⅓ cup blanched almonds, finely chopped
2 tablespoons mild honey
1 tablespoon hot water
1 recipe Plain Rice Pilaf (substitute water for broth and
    see recipe below)

for the Plain Rice Pilaf
2 to 3 tablespoons butter
1 cup long-grain white rice, uncooked
2 cups hot chicken or beef broth
Salt

In a heavy saucepan or casserole melt the butter over moderate heat. Add the rice and cook 2 minutes or until the grains are thoroughly coated with butter but not browned, stirring constantly. Pour in the broth, sprinkle with the salt, and bring to a boil, stirring. Reduce the heat to low. Cover and simmer about 20 minutes or until all the liquid has been absorbed and the rice is tender but still firm to the bite, not mushy. Gently fluff the rice with a fork. Spoon onto a heated serving platter, being careful not to mash it.

TIPS:
You may simmer the rice 15 minutes or until just tender, then stir gently with a fork and place, uncovered, in a preheated 325 degree oven 30 minutes or until the grains are dry and separate. Fluff with a fork every 10 minutes.

In a heavy skillet melt the butter over moderate heat. Add the fruits and nuts and sauté until lightly browned, stirring frequently. Combine the honey and water and add. Cook over low heat about 10 minutes or until the liquid is thickened, stirring occasionally. Arrange the hot pilaf on a serving dish and top with the fruit sauce.

Makes 4 servings

From: *Cuisine of Armenia*

Irish Soda Bread

Ingredients

1 tablespoon butter or margarine
4 cups all-purpose flour
1 teaspoon salt
1 teaspoon baking soda
1 cup buttermilk or 1 cup sweet milk

Rub the butter into the flour. Add the salt and soda, mix all well together by running the dry ingredients through your fingers. Add the buttermilk (or sweet milk) and stir into a soft dough with a wooden spoon. With your floured hands knead lightly into a ball and turn out onto a lightly floured baking sheet. Flatten the dough into a circle 1½ inches thick with the palm of your hand. Make a cross in the center with a floured knife. Bake at 425 degrees for 30 to 35 minutes.

Makes 1 loaf

From: *The Art of Irish Cooking*

 **Gefilte Fish Balls**
Stuffed Fish Balls

Ingredients

3 pounds whole whitefish
2 onions, chopped
2 eggs
½ teaspoon sugar
2 tablespoons matzo meal
½ cup ice water
Salt and pepper
3 carrots, sliced lengthwise
Lemon slices
Parsley

Debone the fish, reserving head and bones. Place bones and head of fish in a pot with 6 cups of water, salt and pepper to taste, and boil over medium heat. Chop remaining fish into small pieces, grind it, and add chopped onion. Carefully add eggs, sugar, matzo meal, ice water, salt and pepper. Chop the mixture very finely. Shape into balls.

Reduce to low heat the pot containing bones and head, gradually put in the fish balls, add the carrots, and cook for 2 hours. Season to taste with additional salt and pepper, and cook for another ½ hour. Discard head, bones and water. Cool fish balls, and arrange on a serving dish. Garnish with lemon slices and parsley.

Makes 6 servings

From: *The Art of Israeli Cooking*

 **Welsh Cheese Pudding**
Pwdin caws pobi Cymreig

Ingredients

4 thick slices bread (without the crusts)
Butter
8 ounces cheddar cheese, grated
½ teaspoon dry mustard
Pepper and cayenne pepper
Pinch of nutmeg
2 cups milk, or half milk and half cream
1 egg

Toast the bread on one side and butter the untoasted side. Place two toast slices, toasted side down, on the bottom of a round, greased, ovenproof dish. On top put half the grated cheese, and half the mustard, pepper, and nutmeg. Then repeat the layer with the toast, toasted side down, and the rest of the cheese on top.

Bring the milk to a boil, add the remaining seasonings, beat the egg and pour the hot milk over it. Pour this over the cheese pudding and let it rest for at least ½ hour, to let the bread soak up the liquid.

Place in a moderate 350 degree oven until it has risen and is light brown on top. Serve quickly.

Makes 2 to 4 servings

From: ***Traditional Food from Wales***

 ## Caerphilly Scones

Though slightly varying from Welsh fare, these scones are a nice addition, most likely hailing from one of the old country house cookery collections. The recipe was sent in to the *Western Mail* when they ran the competition for traditional Welsh dishes, thus resulting in the publication of the recipes by Wales Gas under the title *Croeso Cymreig*.

Parmesan cheese had been popular in Britain since the 16th century and was produced in Britain as a regularity—specifically, in the Gower region.

Ingredients

3 cups all-purpose flour
3 teaspoons baking powder
¼ teaspoon salt
3 tablespoons butter
3 ounces Caerphilly cheese, grated
1 ounce Parmesan cheese, grated
Freshly ground black pepper or a pinch of cayenne
1 cup milk

Sift the flour, baking powder and salt and rub in the butter. Add the grated cheeses with the pepper and mix to a soft dough with the milk (you may not need all of it, just enough to make a soft dough). Roll out at least half an inch thick, stamp out with

11

the largest cutter and bake for 15 to 20 minutes in a hot oven on a greased baking sheet. Serve hot with butter.

TIPS:
Make sure the scones are made thick enough to be soft and moist. Made quite tiny, they are good for buffets or cheese and wine parties.

Makes 2 dozen scones

From: *Traditional Food from Wales*

 # Norwegian Blueberry Omelet

Ingredients

4 eggs, separated
¼ cup cream or milk
¼ teaspoon salt
2 tablespoons butter
¼ cup sugar
1 teaspoon grated lemon peel
Hot Blueberry Sauce (see recipe below)

for the Hot Blueberry Sauce

Combine in a saucepan 1½ cups fresh blueberries (or 1 package, 10-ounce size, frozen blueberries), ½ cup water, 2 tablespoons lemon juice, ⅛ teaspoon salt, and a dash of cinnamon. Stir together ⅔ cup sugar and 1 tablespoon cornstarch; add to blueberry mixture. Cook over moderate heat, stirring until sauce is thickened and smooth.

Beat egg whites until stiff but not dry; set aside. In a large mixing bowl, beat egg yolks until thick and lemon-colored. Beat in cream and salt. Fold in beaten egg whites. Melt butter in heavy frying pan (about 9-inch diameter); turn in eggs. Turn heat to low. Cook very slowly until eggs are golden brown on bottom (about 10 minutes). Place in 350 degree oven, and bake about 10 minutes or until knife inserted in center comes out clean. Loosen omelet from pan. Cut across center. Fold omelet, and turn out onto serving platter. Sprinkle top with sugar mixed with lemon peel. Slip under broiler for a few moments until sugar melts and browns slightly. Pour some of the blueberry sauce over omelet. Serve immediately. Pass remaining blueberry sauce.

Makes 4 servings

From: **The Best of Scandinavian Cooking:**
Danish, Norwegian and Swedish

 ## Swedish Pancakes with Lingonberries

Ingredients

1 cup all-purpose flour
2 teaspoons sugar
¼ teaspoon salt
3 eggs
2 to 3 cups milk
About ⅓ cup butter
Lingonberries or strawberry preserves

Sift flour, measure, and sift again with sugar and salt into mixing bowl. In another bowl, beat together eggs and milk. Gradually stir egg-milk mixture into dry ingredients; beat until smooth. Allow to stand 2 hours. Heat Swedish pancake pan (or crêpe pan or shallow frying pan—no larger than 8 inches

13

in diameter); butter well. Beat batter again. Pour 1 tablespoon batter into each pan section (or just enough batter in crêpe pan or frying pan to cover bottom of pan when tilted). Bake over medium heat until golden brown on the bottom, dry-looking on top; turn and brown on second side. (Stir batter occasionally as you cook pancakes.) Place pancakes on very hot platter; serve immediately with lingonberries or strawberry preserves.

Makes 4 servings

From: ***The Best of Scandinavian Cooking:***
        Danish, Norwegian and Swedish

 ## Risotto alla Milanese

Ingredients

1 chunk of bone marrow
1 onion, chopped
3 tablespoons butter
2½ cups rice
4 cups meat stock
Salt and pepper
Dash of saffron
Cheese, grated (for sprinkling)

Cut the bone marrow into pieces and place in a large pot, where you plan to cook your risotto. Add a chopped onion and a spoonful of butter. Simmer slowly until golden brown. Drop in the rice, mixing with a wooden spoon. Let the rice soak in the butter. On the side bring to a boil meat stock. Add part of it to the rice. Let it cook, adding the broth gradually, when needed. Season with salt and pepper to taste. Add saffron, butter and

14

grated cheese. Do not overcook. Serve with grated cheese sprinkled over it.

Makes 4 to 6 servings

From: *Old Warsaw Cookbook*
   (Italy)

 **Gnocchi**

Ingredients

4 pounds potatoes
3¾ cups all-purpose flour
Salt
2 eggs
Tomato sauce (optional)
Melted butter
Cheese, grated

Cook clean, unpeeled potatoes, until soft. Peel them. Pass through a strainer. Place the flour on a board, add the mashed potatoes, salt and eggs. Knead well together. Cut a small piece of dough. Roll out with your hands until 1 inch thick. Cut strips 1½ inches long with a knife. With your finger shape each piece around so that they are thinner in the middle, forming a canoe-like shape. Drop them into rapidly boiling, salted water. Let them float, and boil a few moments. Drain. Serve with tomato sauce or melted butter and grated cheese.

Makes 4 servings

From: *Old Warsaw Cookbook*
   (Italy)

Stuffed Grapevine Leaves
Yalanci Dolma

Ingredients

6 cups water
1 jar (16 ounces) grapevine leaves
2 large onions, coarsely grated
1 cup rice
3 tablespoons black currants
2 tablespoons pignolia nuts
¼ cup chopped fresh mint
¼ cup chopped parsley (save stems)
¼ cup chopped dill (save stems)
2 tablespoons lemon juice
⅔ cup olive oil
1 teaspoon sugar
1 tablespoon allspice
Salt
2 cups unseasoned chicken broth or water
2 lemons, cut into wedges

Place 6 cups water in a saucepan and bring to a boil. Unroll leaves and place in boiling water. Boil for 2 minutes. Carefully take leaves out with a perforated kitchen spoon and place in a colander to drain. Separate leaves one by one without breaking, remove stem and place around the rim of the colander.

Put onions into a mixing bowl. Add rice, currants, nuts, mint, parsley, dill, lemon juice, oil, sugar, allspice, and salt. Mix well.

Put parsley and dill stems at the bottom of a heavy saucepan.

Take a vine leaf into your left-hand palm, rough side up and the stem end toward you. Place 1 teaspoon of rice mixture, a little more if the leaf is large, on the stem end. Fold stem end over and then fold both sides securely. Roll to end of leaf.

Arrange rolled dolmas in saucepan over dill and parsley stems in close rows. After the first layer, start a new layer until all dolmas are rolled.

Pour over broth or water. Cover dolmas with wax paper and place a plate over the wax paper to give weight during cooking. Cover and cook over medium heat until rice is tender and all the water is absorbed, about 1 hour. If necessary, more broth or water may be added.

Remove from heat and cool, covered.

Arrange dolmas on a serving platter. Decorate with lemon wedges.

Serve cold as hors d'oeuvres. Also very good as a first course.

TIPS:
Allow 4 per person as a first course.
Allow 2 per person as hors d'oeuvres.

Makes 40 dolmas

From: *The Art of Turkish Cooking*

 # Norfolk Dumplings

Set a little dough made with:
½ ounce yeast
1 teaspoon castor sugar
A little milk
½ cup hot water
3¾ cups all-purpose flour

Cream the yeast and sugar together, then mingle the milk and water and pour onto the yeast. Put the flour in a basin, make a well in the center, and pour in the milk and yeast. Mix into a dough, and allow to rise for 1½ to 2 hours. Then knead well, and form into dumplings. Let these stand for 10 minutes. Then plunge them into boiling water, and let them boil for 20 minutes. They must be dished immediately, and served lightly torn at the top with two forks. They are usually eaten with thick brown meat gravy, and sometimes cold with butter and sugar.

Another recipe, dated 1765:
Mix a good thick batter as for pancakes with 1 cup milk, 2 eggs, a little salt, and flour. Have ready a clean saucepan of water boiling, into which drop some of this batter. Be sure that the water boils fast, and boil for 2 or 3 minutes; then throw them into a sieve to drain the water away. Then turn them into a dish and stir a lump of fresh butter into them. Delicious when served hot.

Makes 4 servings

From: *Traditional Food from England*

Savoury Pudding
Stuffing

This is served with goose or duck, and sometimes with roast pork.

Ingredients

Bread
1 tablespoon sage, finely chopped
3 large onions
⅔ cup flour
Salt and pepper
1 egg
1 cup milk

Break up ½ loaf of bread into a basin, and add to the sage. Cut up and boil the 3 onions, and drain them. Chop these up small and mix with the flour. Add a little salt and pepper to taste, and then add 1 egg mixed with the milk. The mixture should be rather stiff. Put into a pudding tin and make level with a spoon (there should be a little shortening in the tin before the mixture is put in). Bake for ½ hour at 350 degrees.

Makes 4 servings

From: *Traditional Food from England*

 **Worcester Sauce**
Worcestershire Sauce

Ingredients

2 cups brown vinegar
3 tablespoons walnut ketchup
2 tablespoons essence anchovy
2 tablespoons soy
¼ teaspoon cayenne
2 shallots, finely chopped
A little salt

Mix the ingredients and cork closely in a large bottle, shake it two or three times a day. Leave overnight. Strain and bottle for use.

Serving size dependent upon use.

From: *Traditional Food from England*

Cornish Pasty

Ingredients

1 pound shortcrust pastry
1 pound lean mutton, trimmed
3 large potatoes, chopped
2 medium onions, chopped
2 medium carrots, chopped
Pinch chopped parsley
Pinch chopped fresh herbs
Salt and pepper

Make the pastry and let chill for about an hour before using. Chop up the meat finely, mix in the chopped vegetables with the meat, herbs and season well. Roll out pastry to a large round. Place meat and vegetable mixture in the center. Bring over one side of the pastry to form a half round. Crimp edges and glaze with milk. Bake in a moderately hot oven for 1 hour. Filling for a Cornish pasty should always be raw.

This Cornish pasty can be made as one large one or several small ones. In Cornwall they were eaten by the Tin and Copper miners at "Crib" time.

Makes 4 to 6 servings

From: *Celtic Cookbook*

21

Georgia's Special Spinach Pie
Spanakopita

Ingredients

4 (10 ounce) packages frozen spinach leaves
1 cup olive oil, divided
1 large onion, finely chopped
1 bunch scallions, chopped
½ cup fresh chopped dill
½ cup fresh chopped parsley
4 large eggs
½ pound crumbled feta cheese
½ cup grated kefalotyri or romano cheese
Salt and pepper
3¾ cups fillo dough

Preheat oven to 350 degrees. Thaw the spinach and squeeze it dry with your hands. Chop into small pieces. Make sure the spinach is thoroughly absent of water. Heat ½ cup olive oil in a medium saucepan. Add the onion, scallions, dill, and the parsley and sauté for 5 minutes. Add the spinach and stir all together. Lower the heat and let simmer for 15 minutes. Take the saucepan off the stove and transfer the mixture to a large bowl. Let cool for 20 minutes.

In a medium bowl, beat the eggs and stir in the feta cheese. Add to the spinach mixture and sprinkle with the kefalotyri (or romano) cheese, salt and pepper to taste, and mix all the ingredients. Oil the bottom of a medium-size (9 × 13 × 2½-inch) baking pan and line with 8 sheets of the fillo dough, brushing each fillo sheet with oil.

Add the spinach mixture and spread evenly in the pan. Fold any overhanging fillo into the pan. Brush each of the remaining fillo sheets with oil and place on top of the spinach mixture. Trim any excess and brush the top of the spinach mixture. Trim any excess and brush the top with more oil. Score the top into squares; do not cut all the way down. Sprinkle with water and bake for 35 to 40 minutes. Remove the pie from the oven and let cool. Cut into pieces and serve hot or cold.

Makes 12 servings

TIPS:
For individual spinach pies, cut the fillo dough into five strips and brush with oil. Put 1 teaspoon of the spinach mixture at one end of the piece of the fillo. Fold up in the shape of a triangle (as you would a flag). Grease a cookie sheet and place pies 1 inch apart. Brush tops with oil. Bake for 15 to 30 minutes.

Makes 3 dozen

From: *Best of Greek Cuisine: Cooking with Georgia*

Serbian Vegetable Caviar
Srpski Avjar

Ingredients

5 large whole green peppers
2 medium whole eggplants
Salt and pepper
5 cloves garlic, minced
4 tablespoons lemon juice
1 cup vegetable oil
3 tablespoons minced parsley

Place whole green peppers and eggplants into a baking pan and bake them in a 500 degree oven. Remove peppers after 25 minutes and set them aside. Continue baking eggplants until tender—about 10 to 15 minutes longer—and remove from oven. To loosen the skins of the eggplants, wrap them in a damp towel for 10 minutes. Peel peppers by pulling off skin; remove ribs and seeds. Dice peppers and place them in a glass or china bowl. Peel and dice eggplants, squeezing them dry with a towel. Place them in the bowl with the peppers. Add salt, pepper, and garlic to taste. Then add lemon juice and oil, and mix well. Refrigerate 1 to 2 hours. Garnish with parsley before serving.

Makes 4 to 6 servings

From: *All Along the Danube*
        (Serbia)

Bosnian Stuffed Cabbage Rolls

Ingredients

1 large head of cabbage
4 cups hot water
1 teaspoon salt
1 pound very lean ground chuck
½ cup cooked rice
4 tablespoons bread crumbs
4 tablespoons light cream
1 egg
¼ teaspoon black pepper
¼ teaspoon oregano
¼ teaspoon tarragon
½ cup chicken broth
⅔ cup of your favorite tomato and meat sauce
     (spaghetti sauce)
½ cup catsup
3 tablespoons butter or margarine
½ cup finely ground Parmesan cheese

Preheat oven to 450 degrees. Core the cabbage. Place it into a pot and pour hot water over it. Add salt and bring to a boil. Simmer cabbage for 15 minutes. Drain and let cool. In a bowl, combine ground chuck, rice, bread crumbs, cream, egg, pepper, oregano and tarragon. Blend well, preferably with your hands. Gently separate cabbage leaves. Cut the larger leaves in two. Cut off the thick center stem. The finished rolls should not be over 2½ inches long. Place about 1 tablespoon of meat mixture on the edge of a cabbage leaf, tuck in the sides, and roll up tightly. Butter a baking dish well and place the rolls close together into dish. Pour chicken broth over rolls; then pour on tomato sauce and catsup. Distribute the sauce evenly over the rolls. Dot with butter. Bake in a preheated 400 degree oven for 45 minutes. Sprinkle with Parmesan cheese and bake for 5 minutes longer. Serve hot.

Makes 16 to 20 rolls

From: *All Along the Danube*
        (Bosnia)

 # Montenegro Omelet

for the Omelet
8 eggs
3 tablespoons light cream
½ teaspoon salt
⅛ teaspoon white pepper
¼ teaspoon thyme
3 tablespoons butter

Beat eggs with cream along with salt, white pepper, and thyme. Melt butter in a 9-inch skillet. Cook omelet until the underside is golden brown. Place a large plate over the skillet and turn the omelet upside down onto the plate. Scrape any bits of egg from skillet. If necessary, add 1 tablespoon of butter to the skillet. Slide omelet back into skillet uncooked side down. Cook until eggs are set. Cut into 6 wedges and serve with the sauce.

for the **Montenegro Sauce**
3 tablespoons olive oil
1 tablespoon butter
2 cloves garlic, crushed
1 medium onion,
finely chopped
1 green pepper, finely chopped
2 ribs celery, finely chopped
1 can (16-ounce) whole tomatoes, drained and chopped
1 teaspoon salt
⅛ teaspoon red hot pepper flakes
½ cup red wine
2 tablespoons brandy

In a large skillet, heat oil and butter, add garlic, onion, green pepper, and celery, and cook until vegetables are limp but not brown. Add tomatoes and salt and hot pepper. Cook, stirring occasionally, for 5 minutes. Add wine; stir, and cook, covered, over low heat for 10 minutes. Uncover; add brandy and cook, stirring occasionally, for 15 minutes.

Makes 6 servings

From: ***All Along the Danube***
(Serbia)

27

Seafood Cocktail Sandwich
Emparedados

Ingredients

1½ cups cooked shrimp, lobster, or crab meat
⅛ teaspoon Tabasco
3 tablespoons minced onions
2 tablespoons minced parsley
2 tablespoons mayonnaise
12 thin slices white bread
1 cup milk
2 eggs
½ cup all-purpose flour
½ teaspoon salt
Fat (for deep frying)

Chop together until very fine the seafood, Tabasco, onions, and parsley; blend in the mayonnaise. Trim the bread and cut in half. Dry in the oven without browning. Dip lightly in the milk (reserve leftover milk) and spread half the pieces with the seafood mixture. Make sandwiches, pressing the edges together.

Beat together the eggs, flour, salt, and remaining milk. Dip the sandwiches in the batter. Heat the fat to 370 degrees and fry the sandwiches until browned. Drain and serve hot.

Makes 12 sandwiches

**From: *The Art of South American Cookery*
(Chile)**

Baked Eggs
Huevos al Horno

Ingredients

6 Uneeda biscuits (crackers)
¼ cup olive oil
½ cup chopped onions
¾ cup chopped green peppers
1½ cups canned tomatoes
1½ teaspoons salt
½ teaspoon freshly ground black pepper
2 hard-boiled eggs, chopped
6 raw eggs
1 tablespoon minced parsley

Roll the crackers into crumbs. Heat the oil in a skillet; sauté the onions and green peppers for 5 minutes. Add the tomatoes, salt, and pepper. Cook over low heat for 10 minutes. Stir in the chopped eggs and cracker crumbs; then carefully break the eggs into the sauce. Sprinkle with the parsley. Bake in a 350 degree oven for 8 minutes or until eggs are set. If you prefer, divide the sauce among individual baking dishes before adding the eggs.

Makes 4 to 6 servings

From: ***The Art of South American Cookery***
(Ecuador)

Corn-Meal Pudding
Pudín de Maíz

Ingredients

2 tablespoons olive oil
¾ cup chopped onions
½ cup chopped green peppers
1 pound ground beef
2 teaspoons salt, divided
¼ teaspoon dried ground chili peppers
½ cup seedless raisins
½ cup sliced black olives
4 egg yolks
1½ cups corn kernels
1 teaspoon sugar
4 egg whites, stiffly beaten

Preheat oven to 400 degrees.

Heat the oil in a skillet; sauté the onions and green peppers for 5 minutes. Mix in the meat, 1¼ teaspoons salt, and the chili peppers until browned. Add the raisins and olives. Turn into a greased 1½-quart casserole dish.

Beat the egg yolks and remaining salt; stir in the corn and sugar. Fold in the egg whites. Heap over the meat mixture. Bake for 20 minutes, or until puffed and browned.

Makes 4 to 6 servings

**From: *The Art of South American Cookery*
(Paraguay)**

Corn Tamales
Humitas de Choclo

Ingredients

4 cups canned corn kernels
¾ cup minced onions
1 cup chopped tomatoes
1½ teaspoons salt
¼ teaspoon dried ground chili peppers
2 tablespoons minced parsley
2 tablespoons olive oil

Mix all the ingredients together. Cut 12 (6-inch) squares of aluminum foil and divide the mixture among them in the center of the foil. Roll up and twist ends to seal. Cook in boiling water for 45 minutes. Drain and serve in the foil. If you prefer, turn mixture into a buttered baking dish. Cover and bake in a 375 degree oven for 25 minutes.

Makes 6 servings

**From: *The Art of South American Cookery*
(Colombia)**

Potato-Cheese Croquettes
Patatas Rellenos con Queso

Ingredients

3 cups mashed potatoes or 2 envelopes instant
    mashed potatoes
2 egg yolks
1½ teaspoons chili powder
¼ pound cream cheese
1 egg, beaten
1 cup dry bread crumbs
Fat (for deep frying)

If instant mashed potatoes are used, prepare the potatoes as package directs, using only ¾ the amount of liquid. Beat in the egg yolks and chili powder. Taste for seasoning. Shape into 1½-inch balls. Make a depression in each and place a teaspoon of cream cheese in it. Cover with the potatoes; roll in the egg and then in the bread crumbs.

Heat the fat to 370 degrees. Fry a few balls at a time until browned. Drain well.

Makes 12 croquettes

From: **The Art of South American Cookery**
      (Bolivia)

Salads

Curried Chicken Salad, Galley Bay

Ingredients

1 pound cooked chicken, diced
1 fresh pineapple, diced
1 head lettuce
2 dozen raisins
2 tablespoons chutney
1 tablespoon shredded coconut
Curried mayonnaise (see recipe below)

for the Curried mayonnaise
2 egg yolks
½ teaspoon prepared mustard
Salt and pepper
½ cup olive oil
1 to 2 teaspoons lemon or lime juice, or vinegar

Beat together egg yolks, mustard and seasonings. Gradually beat in oil, a little at a time, until mixture is thick and creamy; then add lemon or lime juice, or vinegar, a few drops at a time, until the required consistency is obtained.

Combine 2 parts chicken with 1 part pineapple and arrange on a bed of lettuce. Surround with small helpings of raisins, chutney and shredded coconut. Pour enough mayonnaise over chicken and pineapple to coat thickly. Thin mayonnaise with 2 tablespoons boiling water if necessary.

Makes 4 to 6 servings

From: *Cooking the Caribbean Way*
(Antigua)

Savoury Banana Salad

Ingredients

1 head lettuce
1 package (3 ounces) cream cheese
1 teaspoon chopped nuts
4 bananas
1 dozen strawberries
(2 dozen if wild)
1 carton yogurt, unsweetened

Wash and dry lettuce, arrange in individual bowls. Shape cheese into balls about the size of marbles, roll in chopped nuts. Peel and cut bananas lengthwise, place in each bowl. Hull strawberries, cut in half and decorate each bowl with a few. Serve with plain yogurt as a dressing.

Makes 4 to 6 servings

From: ***Cooking the Caribbean Way***
(Tortola)

# Breadfruit Salad

Ingredients

1 breadfruit, boiled and cut into
     small pieces
3 sticks celery, chopped finely
1 large mild onion, chopped finely
Oil
Vinegar
Salt and pepper

Mix the breadfruit, celery and onion. Moisten with oil and vinegar, using 2 parts oil to 1 part vinegar. Season well with salt and pepper and serve chilled.

Makes 4 to 6 servings

From: ***Cooking the Caribbean Way***
       (Grand Cayman)

 # Australian Salad

Ingredients

Thinly sliced firm tomatoes	Cold cooked string beans
Short celery sticks	Small boiled baby potatoes
Grated carrot	(cold with butter)
Thinly sliced cucumber	Sliced boiled egg
Beet root	Gherkins
Thinly sliced orange	Pickled onions
Thin slices of banana	Canned salmon
1 or 2 pieces of apple	Raisins
Fresh pineapple squares	Avocado
Fresh whole lettuce leaves	Roast beef
Parsley	Slices of chicken
Grated cheese	Ham
Cold cooked peas	Other desired cold cut meats

Use as wide a variety of fresh garden vegetables as you can find. The Australian salad is most often served with a few thin slices of cold cuts, such as roast beef, ham, German sausage, chicken, or a little potted meat. Naturally, these cold dishes are most popular in summertime, especially to clean up any leftover turkey from Christmas dinner. The cold cuts are usually arranged flat on one side of the plate, nestling against various ingredients, with crisp lettuce on the outside of the plate. Thin slices of orange, split and twisted are common—intended to be eaten as well as for decoration.

Makes many servings

From: *Good Food from Australia*

Chicken & Vegetable Salad

Ingredients

¾ pound chicken breast, cooked and diced
2 large potatoes, peeled and diced
2 hard-boiled eggs, peeled
2 tablespoons mayonnaise
Salt and pepper
1 Kirby cucumber, peeled and sliced
2 plum tomatoes, sliced
2 tablespoons minced coriander
2 scallions (green part), minced

Carefully blend chicken with potatoes, taking care not to mash the potatoes. Coarsely chop 1 of the hard-boiled eggs and add to the mixture. Fold in mayonnaise and sprinkle with salt and pepper to taste. Slice the second hard-boiled egg. Mound salad on a plate and cover it with a decorative pattern of tomato, cucumber and egg slices. Sprinkle with minced coriander and scallions. Serve at room temperature.

Makes 4 to 5 servings

From: *The Cooking of Uzbekistan*

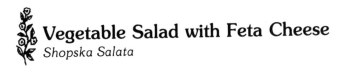

Vegetable Salad with Feta Cheese
Shopska Salata

Ingredients

4 peppers
2 onions
3 tomatoes
2 small cucumbers
¼ cup minced fresh parsley
3 tablespoons olive oil
1 tablespoon vinegar
2 dashes salt
½ pound feta cheese

Roast the peppers over charcoal or in a hot pan,* turning them by the stem until their skin is burned and they become very soft inside. Put them in a pot and cover well for a couple of minutes, so that the skins will be easy to peel off. Peel skins off, cut off the stems, clean out the seeds, and cut the peppers into ½ × 1-inch pieces.

Cut onions lengthwise into crescents and add to peppers. Dice tomatoes and cucumbers. Add to peppers and onions. Add minced parsley, oil, vinegar, and salt. Mix. Sprinkle crumbled feta cheese on top.

*TIPS:
Do not cook peppers in an oven or a microwave which will ruin their fibers.

Makes 4 to 6 servings

From: *Traditional Bulgarian Cooking*

Tuna or Swordfish Salad
Insalata tat-Tonn jew Pixxispad

Ingredients

3 ounces pickled onions
1 large onion, peeled and chopped or 3 large shallots,
    chopped
2 to 3 tablespoons capers, well-drained and rinsed
3 to 4 tablespoons green olives, well-drained and rinsed
2 hard-boiled eggs, shelled, peeled, and chopped
3 to 4 large potatoes, peeled, boiled, chilled, and sliced
2 to 3 baked swordfish or tuna streaks, deboned, flaked,
    and chilled
Salt and freshly ground black pepper
Lettuce wedges for 4 persons
Olive oil and vinegar for drizzling or vinaigrette
3 to 4 large ripe tomatoes, sliced
Lemon wedges
Loaf of crusty bread

In a large bowl, toss pickled onion, onion, capers, olives, hard-boiled eggs, and potatoes. Add fish. Toss again. Add salt and pepper to taste. Place each of 4 portions of the fish salad on a lettuce wedge. Drizzle with olive oil and vinegar. Garnish with tomato slices and lemon wedges. Refrigerate until ready to use.

Serve well-chilled with a loaf of crusty bread.

Makes 4 servings

From: *Taste of Malta*

Baked Eggplant Salad

Ingredients

2 pounds eggplant
10 garlic cloves, chopped
3 tablespoons chopped parsley
½ teacup pure olive oil
½ teacup vinegar
Salt
Pepper

Grill or bake the whole eggplants until tender. Peel eggplants and mash; mix well with garlic, parsley, olive oil, vinegar, salt and pepper in a porcelain or earthenware bowl. Serve cold in small dishes, sprinkling the salad with olive oil.

Makes 6 servings

From: *The Best of Albanian Cooking:*
Favorite Family Recipes

Potato Salad with Wine
Salatka z kartofli z winem

Ingredients

1 pound small potatoes (with jackets)
3 tablespoons dry white wine
1 small whole unpeeled celeraic
½ cup vinaigrette
Chopped dill
Chopped parsley
Chives

Cook the potatoes in jackets until tender. Peel under cold running water, slice while hot, and sprinkle with the wine. Let stand 30 minutes. meanwhile, cook the celeraic in boiling water until tender, peel under cold running water, and sieve it. Mix sieved celeraic well with the vinaigrette and toss with potatoes. Sprinkle with chopped dill, parsley, and chives.

Makes 4 to 6 servings

From: *Polish Heritage Cookery*

 **Ensalada de Aguacate**
Avocado Salad

Ingredients

1 large avocado, cut into strips
1 medium onion, sliced and separated
4 dried red chilies, ground
2 limes

Place the avocado strips on a platter or individual serving dish. Add the sliced onion rings. Add the dried red chili, to taste. Squeeze plenty of lime juice over the top.

Makes 4 to 6 servings

From: ***Mayan Cooking: Recipes from the Sun Kingdoms of Mexico***
(Maya)

 **Warsaw Salad**

Ingredients

2 cups beets, cooked or canned
2 cups kidney beans, cooked or canned
2 cups peas, cooked or canned
3 pickles, diced
1 can crab meat
3 scallions, chopped
1 cup prepared mayonnaise
½ cup sour cream
1 tablespoon mustard
1 hard-boiled egg
Carrots (to garnish)
Radishes (to garnish)

Mix the diced, cooked or canned vegetables (beets, kidney beans, peas) with diced pickles, can of crab meat and scallions. Prepare mayonnaise and combine with sour cream and mustard. Pour over the salad. Garnish with a quartered egg, strips of carrots and rose radishes.

Makes 6 servings

From: *Old Warsaw Cookbook*

Ukrainian Zakuska

Ingredients

½ pound beets, cooked
and peeled
½ pound cabbage
½ pound apples
1 tablespoon salt
½ cup mayonnaise
1 lemon
½ pound ham
½ pound fillet of goose
or turkey breast
2 eggs, boiled
2 cucumbers
3 tomatoes
1 bunch parsley

Cut beets, cabbage and apples into straws. Stir chopped cabbage with salt. Press out moisture and mix with cut apples and beets. Combine mayonnaise and juice of lemon and pour over beet mixture. Add small pieces of ham and fillet of goose or turkey breast. Decorate with sliced eggs, cucumbers and tomatoes. Sprinkle with salt and chopped fresh parsley.

Makes 6 servings

From: *The Best of Ukrainian Cuisine*

Apple, Cheese & Nuts Salad
Salata de Mere, Brânza, si Nuci

Ingredients

4 apples, peeled and cored
½ pounds cascaval cheese*
2 ounces chopped walnuts
1 teaspoon granulated sugar
½ teaspoon salt
2 teaspoons mayonnaise
4 lettuce leaves

Grate apples and cheese. Mix together in a bowl. Add walnuts, sugar, and salt. Mix. Add mayonnaise, and mix everything well together.

In each individual salad bowl, place a lettuce leaf. Place a scoop of salad on the lettuce.

*TIPS:
If you cannot find cascaval cheese, you can use any hard ewe milk cheese, or a sharp cheddar cheese will do well for this salad.

Makes 4 servings

From: *Taste of Romania*

Greek Salad
Eliniki Salada

Ingredients

3 large tomatoes, sliced
2 small cucumbers, sliced
1 medium onion, sliced
1 Italian sweet pepper, sliced
3 to 4 scallions, chopped
1 teaspoon dried oregano
Salt and pepper
½ cup crumbled feta cheese
5 to 6 black olives
½ cup olive oil
3 tablespoons white vinegar

Place the vegetables in a large salad bowl in the following order: tomatoes, cucumbers, onion, pepper and scallions. Sprinkle the oregano, and salt and pepper to taste on the vegetables. Crumble the feta cheese on top and add the olives.

Mix together the oil and vinegar and pour it over the entire mixture of vegetables in the salad bowl.

Makes 4 servings

From: *Best of Greek Cuisine: Cooking with Georgia*

 Cauliflower Salad

Ingredients

5 cups cauliflower florets
6 cups water
1½ bay leaves
4 peppercorns
Salt

for the Salad

In a two quart saucepan, boil cauliflower in water with the bay leaves, peppercorn, and salt to taste for 10 minutes, or until tender. Drain and set aside, but keep warm.

for the Dressing

⅔ cup water
5 tablespoons vinegar
5 tablespoons oil
1 medium onion, minced
1 teaspoon sugar
Salt and pepper
3 tablespoons minced dill

Blend all ingredients thoroughly. Place cauliflower in an airtight container and pour dressing over the florets. Refrigerate for at least 4 hours before serving.

Makes 6 servings

From: ***All Along the Danube***
(Czech)

Guacamole Salad
Ensalada de Guacamole

Ingredients

2 avocados
1 cup peeled, diced tomatoes
2 hard-boiled eggs, diced
½ cup sliced, stuffed olives
¼ cup minced onions
⅓ cup olive oil
2 tablespoons cider vinegar
1¼ teaspoons salt
¼ teaspoon dried ground chili peppers
Lettuce
4 slices crisp bacon, crumbled

Peel and dice the avocados; mix with the tomatoes, eggs, olives, onions, oil, vinegar, salt, and chili peppers. Heap on lettuce leaves and sprinkle the bacon on top.

Makes 4 to 6 servings

From: ***The Art of South American Cookery***
(Mexico)

Soups

Zambian Groundnut Soup

Ingredients

1 large tomato, peeled and cut in eighths
1 large onion, cut in eighths
1 large potato, peeled and cut in eighths
2 tablespoons rice
Soup bones, if available
Salt
2¼ cups water
1 cup finely ground unsalted peanuts

Combine the tomato, onion, potato, rice, soup bones, and salt to taste with 2 cups water. Simmer until vegetables are soft. Mix ground peanuts with ¼ cup water and add to pot. Simmer 30 minutes more.

Makes 6 servings

From: ***Best of Regional African Cooking***
(Zambia)

Shrimp Soup

Ingredients

1 pound white fish
6 cups water
½ pound shrimps
1 teaspoon butter
Salt and pepper
2 cloves
Pinch thyme
Strip of lemon or lime peel
1 scallion, chopped
12 tablespoons all-purpose flour
Lime or lemon juice

Put fish in water and bring to a boil. Boil until liquid is reduced to 2 pints, then remove fish. Pick shrimps and pound heads, tails and skins finely. Add these and shrimp meat to fish stock, together with butter, salt, pepper, cloves, thyme, lemon or lime peel, and scallion. Boil for 10 minutes then remove shrimps. Cut into small pieces and leave in a warmed soup tureen. Simmer remaining ingredients for a further 30 minutes. Take out a little of the stock and allow to cool slightly. Mix with enough flour to thicken the soup to taste, return to soup and stir until thickened. Pour over shrimps, add a squeeze of lime or lemon juice and serve hot.

Makes 4 to 6 servings

From: *Cooking the Caribbean Way*
(Jamaica)

53

Okra Soup

Ingredients

½ pound mutton
1 fresh conch or clam (optional)
¼ pound white fish
12 small okra
1 pound potatoes
1 stick celery
1 green corn
1 onion
1 carrot
½ stick butter
2 tablespoons all-purpose flour
1 tablespoon tomato paste or ketchup
8 cups water
Salt and pepper

Mince mutton, conch and white fish and dice the cleaned and prepared vegetables: okra, potatoes, celery, green corn, onion, and carrot. Melt butter and cook meat, fish and vegetables for 5 minutes. Add flour and stir in tomato paste, blending well. Stir in water and keep stirring until soup comes to a boil. Skim. Add salt and pepper and allow to simmer gently for 2 hours.*

*TIPS:
This soup is often served as the only course for a midday meal.

Makes 6 servings

From: ***Cooking the Caribbean Way***
(Dominica)

Caribbean Nut Soup

Ingredients

½ stick butter
3 tablespoons rice flour or chestnut flour
2 cups milk
1 jar yogurt
1 teaspoon salt
8 ounces almonds or cashews
Nuts, ground finely

Melt butter, stir in flour, cook over a low heat for 5 minutes, stirring all the time and taking care the mixture does not brown. Remove from heat, gradually stir in milk. Add the yogurt, salt, almonds or cashews and nuts; stir well and bring to a boil. Lower heat and simmer gently until creamy.

Makes 4 servings

From: ***Cooking the Caribbean Way***
(Gorda)

Cold Sour Milk & Herbs Soup
Chalop

Ingredients

2 cups buttermilk
1 cup plain yogurt
1 cup sour cream
1 cup water
6 Kirby cucumbers, peeled, seeded and diced
10 red radishes, diced
½ cup diced daikon
4 scallions, diced (green and white parts)
2 tablespoons chopped parsley
2 tablespoons chopped dill
2 tablespoons chopped coriander
Salt and pepper

In a large bowl, stir the buttermilk, yogurt and sour cream and water until smooth. Add the diced cucumbers, radishes, daikon and scallion, and stir until smooth. Sprinkle in the herbs and salt and pepper to taste. Chill for at least 3 hours.

Makes 6 servings

From: *The Cooking of Uzbekistan*

 # Orange Consommé

Ingredients

1 large can consommé
Juice of 3 oranges
3 cloves
1 orange, thinly sliced

Bring consommé, juice and cloves to a boil. Serve immediately, decorating individual servings with orange slices.

This soup is equally good served ice cold.

Makes 4 servings

From: ***Cooking the Caribbean Way***
      (Haiti)

 # Chilled Yogurt & Cucumber Soup
Jajik

This is a light and refreshing soup of inspired simplicity, renowned throughout the Middle East.

Ingredients

2 medium cucumbers (about ½ pound each)
4 cups plain yogurt
1 cup ice water
Salt
2 tablespoons finely chopped fresh mint leaves
2 tablespoons finely chopped scallions, including 2 inches of the green tops
4 ice cubes or ¾ cup crushed ice

Peel the cucumbers and cut lengthwise into eighths. Cut out the seeds if too large and discard. Slice the cucumbers crosswise into ¼-inch pieces.

Pour the yogurt into a deep bowl and stir with a large spoon until smooth. Add the ice water and blend gently but thoroughly. Add the cucumbers and salt and stir well. Taste for seasoning and refrigerate for several hours until thoroughly chilled.

Just before serving, sprinkle the soup with the mint and scallions. Serve in individual soup bowls, adding 1 ice cube to each bowl. (If using crushed ice, add with mint and scallions.)

Makes 4 servings

 Variation: **Matsnabrdosh**

The Caucasian variation of *jajik* is prepared by mixing equal amounts of yogurt and ice water and adding diced cucumbers, sliced hard-boiled eggs, chopped scallions, minced fresh herbs (dill, parsley, coriander), and salt to taste. *Matsnabrdosh* is served cold, with an ice cube or two added to each serving.

From: *The Cuisine of Armenia*

Spinach Soup
Pinaattikeitto

This soup is often made with young nettles, picked with gloves on and blanched in boiling water to remove the sting.

Ingredients

1 pound fresh spinach or 1 package frozen spinach
2 tablespoons butter
2 tablespoons all-purpose flour
4 cups vegetable or chicken broth, or water
¼ teaspoon pepper
⅛ teaspoon ground nutmeg
Salt
1 egg yolk
¼ cup heavy cream
1 hard-boiled egg

Wash the spinach well, place in a saucepan, cover tightly and let cook about 5 minutes, until softened. Remove and chop finely.

In another saucepan melt the butter, stir in the flour and let cook briefly. Gradually whisk in the broth or water, let cook for a few minutes, and add the chopped spinach, pepper and nutmeg. Let simmer about 5 minutes and remove from heat. Add salt to taste.

In a small bowl mix the egg yolk with the cream, add about a cupful of the soup and then stir this back into the soup. Heat almost to a boil but do not let boil. Remove from heat. Serve in soup bowls, garnished with sliced or chopped hard-boiled egg.

Makes 4 servings

From: *The Best of Finnish Cooking*

Prazsky Goulash

This is a simple, meat intensive stew that combines beef with good-quality frankfurters and plenty of onions and is spiced with paprika and caraway.

Ingredients

2 tablespoons lard or vegetable oil
1½ pounds stewing beef
2 large onions, chopped
2 cloves garlic, mashed
1 tablespoon paprika (for sprinkling)
5 cups water
2 tablespoons tomato purée
½ teaspoon marjoram
1 tablespoon crushed caraway seeds
Salt
Freshly ground black pepper
4 frankfurters, sliced thick
2 tablespoons butter
2 tablespoons all-purpose flour

Heat the lard or oil in a large pot on medium-high. When quite hot, put in the beef and brown it all over. Add the onions and garlic and fry, stirring occasionally, until almost golden. Sprinkle on the paprika and fry for another couple of minutes. Add about 5 cups of water. Stir in the tomato purée. Mix in the marjoram and caraway seeds and season well with salt and freshly ground black pepper to taste. Bring to a boil, cover, reduce heat, and let simmer until tender, about 1½ hours.

A few minutes before serving, add the frankfurters and heat through. To thicken the sauce, make a roux by melting the butter in a frying pan, then adding the flour and frying for 3 to 4 minutes; stir the roux into the stew and cook for a couple of minutes.

Serve with bread, potatoes, or dumplings and a green salad.

Makes 4 to 6 servings

From: *The Best of Czech Cooking*

 **Beer Soup**
Pivní Polévka

This is a delicious soup made with bread and fortified by some beer.*

Ingredients

½ loaf of dark bread
1 bottle of good beer
6 cups beef broth
1 tablespoon crushed caraway seeds
Salt
2 eggs
1 egg yolk
½ cup heavy cream

Cut the bread into small cubes and place in a bowl. Cover bread with beer and soak for a few minutes.

Bring the broth to a boil in a large pot. Add the beer and bread mixture. Cook for just a few minutes. Let cool for several minutes, then process in food processor or mash through a sieve.

Put the puréed soup back on the element and bring to a slow boil. Add the caraway seeds, salt to taste, whole eggs and the yolk. Take off the heat and mix in the cream.

*TIPS:
Choose a good, strong flavored beer to use with a tasty broth. If available, a suggested beer is Czech Pilsen.

Makes 4 to 6 servings

From: *The Best of Czech Cooking*

 **Cold Raspberry Soup**
Hideg Málnaleves

Ingredients

1 pound raspberries
½ cup granulated sugar
Handful of Rice Krispies or popcorn
        (for sprinkling)

Wash, clean, and crush fresh raspberries. Cover with sugar and let stand for several hours. Press through strainer. Chill. Stir before serving. Sprinkle Rice Krispies or popcorn over each serving, to add contrast to soup.

Makes 6 servings

From: *The Art of Hungarian Cooking*

Irish Stew

Ingredients

3 pounds neck of lamb
12 medium potatoes
4 large onions, sliced
Salt and pepper
1 sprig thyme
About 2 cups water

Remove the fat from the meat and cut into 8 to 10 sections through the bone. Do not remove the bone, as this adds flavor. Peel the potatoes and slice 4 of them into thin slices. Leave the rest of the potatoes whole.

Into a saucepan put the thinly sliced potatoes, then a layer of sliced onions, and then the sections of lamb. Season well with the salt and pepper to taste. Add the thyme and another layer of sliced onion. Cover with the remainder of the potatoes, which have been left whole. Season again and add 2 cups of water. Cover the pot with aluminum foil and with a very tight-fitting lid.

Cook in the oven for 2½ hours at 350 degrees or simmer gently over the stove for the same time.

The thinly sliced potatoes at the bottom of the pot should dissolve and thicken the juice, while the potatoes on top retain their shape and remain floury.

Makes 6 servings

From: *The Art of Irish Cooking*

Goulash
Gulyás

This is a favorite dish with Mrs. Willy Pogany, a noted Hungarian hostess. She sets the stage for a dinner with a peasant atmosphere by serving it piping hot from an earthen casserole. With it she serves soft noodles or pinched noodles. With dill pickles, a green salad, dark bread, and good coffee, the meal is complete with or without dessert.

Ingredients

4 pounds beef (chuck or rump), cut in 2-inch pieces
1 cup water
2 strips bacon or salt pork, or 2 tablespoons bacon fat
6 onions, coarsely chopped
3 tablespoons paprika
1½ teaspoons salt
2 green peppers, coarsely chopped

Brown half the beef in its own fat in a large skillet; transfer to a kettle or Dutch oven and repeat with other half. Rinse the skillet with 1 cup of water and add the liquid to the meat. Cover and cook slowly over low heat.

Chop the bacon and fry in skillet; add the onions and brown lightly. stir in the paprika and salt to taste; then combine with the simmering meat. Stir in the uncooked green peppers and continue cooking slowly for about 2 hours or until the meat is tender—not soft.

Makes 8 to 10 servings

From: *The Art of Hungarian Cooking*

Kniedel Soup with Celery
Karpasia

Ingredients

1 to 2 beef bones
1 large onion
1 pound beef, sliced
3 cloves garlic
2 tablespoons chopped celery
Parsley, chopped
1 large summer squash, sliced thinly
1 cup matzo meal
1 teaspoon oil
2 tablespoons ground beef
1 egg
Black pepper
Salt
Juice of 1 lemon

In a saucepan place bones, onion, meat, garlic, most of the celery, parsley and squash. Add 4 cups water and let simmer over low heat. Stew until liquid evaporates and meat is cooked. Add 6 more cups water, and continue to simmer over very low heat with lid on for 1½ hours.

Combine matzo meal with ½ cup lukewarm water, oil and ground beef. Mix well, to an even texture. Add remainder of chopped celery and egg, and continue to mix.

Form 1-inch balls. Drop them into soup and let cook for 20 minutes. Add salt and pepper to taste. Shortly before end of cooking, add lemon juice.

Serve hot with matzos or crackers.

Makes 8 to 10 servings

From: *The Art of Israeli Cooking*

Chinese Watercress Soup

Gwaah Jee Choy Tong

Ingredients

2 ounces minced pork
1 teaspoon cornstarch
½ teaspoon sugar
½ teaspoon pepper
1 tablespoon soya sauce
1 tablespoon vegetable oil
2 slices ginger
1 tablespoon salt
6 cups boiling water
1 pound *gwaah jee choy* (Chinese watercress)*
2 well-beaten eggs

Mix minced pork with cornstarch, sugar, pepper, soya sauce, and vegetable oil. Heat a little oil in a pot, fry ginger and salt for ½ minute, and pour in 6 cups boiling water. Bring water to fresh boil and toss in Chinese watercress, cover pot with lid, and simmer 10 minutes. Then toss in meat mixture. Cover pot, boil 5 minutes, take pot off fire and allow soup to cook in its own heat for 5 minutes. Stir in beaten eggs gently, and when eggs are slightly set, serve.

*TIPS:

Gwaah jee choy, Chinese watercress, called *verdolagas* in Mexico, has a slight vinegar flavor. Its leaves resemble the shape of watermelon seeds, and thus in China it has acquired the name of "Melon seed plant." Unlike the watercress, *gwaah jee choy* seems to be a padded plant saturated with water.

Makes 4 to 6 servings

From: *The Joy of Chinese Cooking*

Flemish Fish Soup
Ghentsche Waterzooie

Ingredients

8 cups water
4 cups dry white wine
2 carrots, diced
1 onion, chopped
5 sprigs of parsley
¼ teaspoon mace
1 bay leaf
4 cloves
Salt and pepper
2 pounds fish (carp, brill or perch *and* eel)
6 small lake fish, or 12 smelts
½ cup heavy cream

Simmer water, wine, carrots, onion, parsley, mace, bay leaf, cloves, and salt and pepper to taste for 20 minutes. Add carp or substitute. Simmer together until fish is cooked. Rub through food mill into kettle. Place the small fish in sieve. Lower sieve into soup and cook until done. Remove fish and reserve. Add cream to soup. Do not allow to boil again.

Serve with thinly sliced round pumpernickel bread sandwiches, well buttered, and place a small whole fish or 2 smelts in each plate. Serves 6 generously.

TIPS:
Freezes very well; reheat in a double boiler.

Makes 6+ servings

From: *A Belgian Cookbook*

Flemish Beer Stew
Carbonnade Flamande

Ingredients

1 pound onions, thinly sliced
4 tablespoons butter
2½ pounds round steak, cubed
1 clove garlic, pressed or crushed
⅛ teaspoon nutmeg
⅛ teaspoon thyme
Salt and pepper
4 cups light beer
2 tablespoons butter kneaded with 2 tablespoons
        all-purpose flour
1 tablespoon granulated sugar

Sauté onions lightly in 2 tablespoons of the butter in deep pan or flameproof casserole. Reserve. In same pot melt remaining butter and brown beef on all sides until it has a very dark color. When done, replace onions, add garlic, nutmeg, thyme, salt and pepper to taste, and then beer. Cover, bring to a boil, reduce heat and simmer for 1½ hours. Remove meat from pan juices and keep hot. Drop butter-flour mixture into juices, add sugar and boil uncovered for 8 minutes over medium heat. Taste, correct seasoning.

Serve with boiled potatoes and drink beer with this delectable dish.

Makes 4 servings

From: *A Belgian Cookbook*

70

 **Danish Cheese Soup**

Ingredients

2 tablespoons butter
¼ cup sliced green onions with tops
2 tablespoons all-purpose flour
2 cups milk
2 cups chicken stock
2 carrots, peeled and cut into ¼-inch cubes
⅓ cup chopped celery
2 cups (about ½ pound) shredded Danish Danbo cheese
      (or other mild-to-medium-sharp natural cheese such
      as Cheddar, Jack, Gouda)
½ teaspoon salt
¼ teaspoon paprika (reserve more for sprinkling)
⅛ teaspoon pepper
2 tablespoons freshly chopped parsley

In a large saucepan, melt butter. Add onions and sauté until limp. Stir in flour, blending to make a smooth paste. Gradually add milk and stock, cooking and stirring to make a smooth, thin sauce. Add carrots, celery, cheese, salt, the ¼ teaspoon paprika, and pepper. Cover soup and simmer 15 minutes or until cheese is melted and vegetables are slightly tender; stir occasionally. Just before serving, add chopped parsley. Sprinkle top of each serving with additional paprika.

Makes 8 first-course or 4 main-course servings

From: *The Best of Scandinavian Cooking*

71

 # Scotch Broth

Ingredients

½ to 1 pound runner of beef (or neck of mutton)
Salt
¼ cup barley
Pepper
1 turnip, diced
1 carrot, diced
1 leek, sliced
1 carrot, grated
4 cups cold water
1 generous teaspoon chopped parsley

Wipe the meat, put it into a pan with sufficient cold water to cover it, add the salt and the barley (thoroughly washed), bring the water to boiling, and skim. Add the pepper and the diced turnips, carrots, and sliced leeks. Simmer for 3 or 4 hours. Add the grated carrot ½ hour before dishing. When ready, lift the meat out, skim the broth, add the chopped parsley, boil, and serve.

TIPS:
If meat is to be served as a separate course, cook blocks of carrot and turnip in the broth. Serve meat and vegetables, pouring a little of the liquor over.

Makes 4 servings

From: *Traditional Food From Scotland*

 **Ukrainian Borsch**

Ingredients

1 pound desired meat, cubed
1 parsley root
½ pound beets
1 pound potatoes
½ cup tomato paste
1 tablespoon vinegar
1 tablespoon pig fat
1 onion, diced
1 tablespoon all-purpose flour, browned
1 pound cabbage, chopped
1 clove garlic, chopped
Salt
1 tablespoon butter
3 bay leaves
¼ teaspoon black pepper
½ pound tomatoes
½ cup sour cream
Handful chopped parsley

Cook chosen meat in 2 quarts water to make bouillon. Clean and shred parsley root and beets thinly in straws. Cut potatoes in cubes and place in pot with beets and sauté with tomato paste, vinegar and pig fat. Brown diced onion and parsley root. Mix with slightly browned flour, add bouillon and bring to boil. Place cut potatoes, cabbage and sautéed beets in bouillon. Add garlic and salt to taste and cook 10 to 15 minutes. Next, add cubed meat browned with flour, bay leaves, black pepper and cook until potatoes and cabbage are tender. Add salted pig fat chopped with garlic to prepared borsch. Cut tomatoes, place in borsch, bring to boil. Cover borsch, when ready, and let it rest for 15 to 20 minutes. Serve with sour cream and chopped parsley.

Makes 6 servings

From: *The Best of Ukrainian Cuisine*

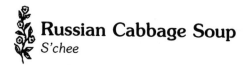 **Russian Cabbage Soup**
S'chee

Ingredients

2 pounds fresh cabbage
2 carrots
2 stalks celery
1 celery knob
3 tomatoes or 1 tablespoon tomato purée
3 medium potatoes
6 or 8 cups white or yellow (or canned) consommé
1 large onion, sliced
3 tablespoons butter (or bacon fat), divided
1 tablespoon all-purpose flour
½ teaspoon salt
1 tablespoon minced parsley
1 tablespoon minced dill
1 cup sour cream

Cut a firm cabbage in quarters, discarding the hard core and any very hard ribs of the leaves. Pour boiling water over the cabbage to scald it; rinse off with cold water and set aside to drain well. Chop coarsely when drained. Cut the carrots and celery in 1-inch pieces; cube the celery knob; peel and seed the tomatoes; cut the potatoes in halves. Add these vegetables (excluding the onion and cabbage) to the consommé and boil up once, then simmer gently. In another pot, simmer sliced onion for 5 minutes in 2 tablespoons of butter or bacon fat. Add the cabbage; cover the pot and braise gently for 20 minutes. Add the consommé to this, a couple of spoonfuls at a time, and continue cooking for 30 minutes. The cabbage should become pinkish in color. Brown the flour in the remaining tablespoon of butter or bacon fat, thicken the soup with this, then add the cabbage and salt. Boil. Cook for 20 minutes.

If you are serving *S'chee* the Russian way, you must have a large tureen well-heated. Slice the meat left from making the consommé. Put the meat in the tureen and sprinkle it with the minced parsley and dill. Pour in the soup and serve meat and soup together, scalding hot. The sour cream is passed at table. When the meat is to be served as a separate course, it is heated in the soup for 20 minutes before serving, then cut up at table.

Makes 4 to 6 servings

From: *The Best of Russian Cooking*

French Onion Soup
Potage á l'Oignon

Ingredients

4 onions
4 tablespoons butter or margarine
5 cups meat stock
Fried or toasted bread
Garlic
Salt and pepper
5 tablespoons grated cheese

Peel and slice the onions. Fry them lightly in butter until golden-brown. Pour the meat stock over the onions and simmer together for 15 minutes. On the side prepare the toast. Rub it with garlic and fry in butter for a moment, just on one side and add salt and pepper to taste. Place the bread in individual serving bowls. Serve the soup very hot and sprinkle generously with grated cheese.

Makes 4 servings

**From: Old Warsaw Cookbook
(France)**

77

Bouillabaise

Ingredients

2 carrots, sliced
2 celery stalks
2 potatoes, cubed
3 tomatoes, sliced
Water (to cover)
Lobster
Crab meat
¼ pound salmon
½ pound eel
¼ pound cod
4 tablespoons olive oil
1 cup white wine
Toasted bread
3 cloves garlic
Salt and pepper
Parsley (to garnish)

Cook the vegetables in water for 5 minutes. On the side, season all the fish, cover with oil and wine, let stand for 10 minutes. Place the fish in vegetable stock and boil rapidly for 10 minutes. Take the lobster out, extract all the lobster meat, and put back in the soup. Toast the bread, rub it with garlic. Garnish with parsley before serving. Serve the bouillabaise with toasted bread.

Makes 6 servings

From: ***Old Warsaw Cookbook***
(France)

78

Minestrone alla Fiorentina

Ingredients

1 large onion, chopped
8 tablespoons olive oil
¼ pound boiled ham, sliced
1 quarter red cabbage, chopped
3 carrots, sliced
3 celery stalks, chopped
Handful of peas
Handful of string beans

2 tablespoons tomato paste
8 cups water
2 cups kidney beans, cooked
Rosemary
Thyme
2 cloves garlic
Salt and pepper
Grated cheese
Croutons of dark bread

Sauté chopped onion in some of the oil. Add sliced ham. Simmer for a moment. Add chopped cabbage along with the carrots, celery, peas, and string beans. Mix a few times. Add tomato paste and stew until the vegetables begin to be tender, then add water and cooked kidney beans. Cook on low heat for 1 hour. On the side, prepare rosemary, thyme, and garlic and fry them in oil, until the garlic becomes golden-brown, then pour this mixture in the minestrone. Flavor with salt and pepper to taste; serve with grated cheese and croutons of dark bread.

TIPS:
Rice or noodles may be substituted for croutons.

Makes 6 servings

From: *Old Warsaw Cookbook*
(Italy)

Swedish Fish Soup

Ingredients

1 carrot
6 stalks celery
6 cups fish bouillon
2 tablespoons chopped parsley
10 peppercorns
3 cloves
1 bay-leaf
1 tablespoon butter
3 tablespoons all-purpose flour
3 tablespoons grated cheese
2 yolks, beaten
Salt

The vegetables (carrots and celery) are put on with the fish bouillon and the parsley, peppercorns, cloves, and bay-leaf. Simmer for 1½ hours in butter. Strain and thicken with flour in the usual manner. The cheese is added last before pouring the soup over the beaten yolks. Add salt to taste and serve very hot. Pieces of fish may be left in for garnish.

Makes 6 servings

From: *Good Food from Sweden*

Gazpacho Andaluz
*Andalusian Cold
Salad Soup*

In the hot summer months, this
summer favorite appears on the
Spanish table daily.

Ingredients

for the Garnish
Finely chopped onion, peppers, cucumber, cured ham,
fried bread cubes, etc., served in separate dishes.

for the Soup
1 small onion
1 cucumber
1 green pepper
6 large tomatoes, peeled and seeded
1 clove garlic
2 cups coarse bread crumbs
Salt
3 tablespoons white wine vinegar
¼ cup olive oil
4 cups cold water
Ice cubes

Chop the onion, cucumber, pepper, tomatoes and garlic,
then mix together with the bread crumbs, salt, vinegar, oil
and water. Put the ingredients into a blender or processor and
blend to a smooth purée. Transfer to serving bowl and place in

81

refrigerator for about 2 hours. Just before serving, add a few ice cubes (and a little more water if desired) and stir well.

The garnishes, consisting of bowls of chopped peppers, tomatoes, cured ham, cucumber, fried bread cubes, etc., are passed around and added to the gazpacho according to individual preference.

Makes 6 to 8 servings

From: *A Spanish Family Cookbook*

Vegetables

Nigerian Spinach Stew

Ingredients

2 pounds spinach or 2 (10-ounce) packages frozen
    chopped spinach, cooked and drained
Meat or fish as desired
½ to 1 teaspoon cayenne
1 tablespoon ground tomatoes
1 tablespoon ground onion
¼ to ½ cup palm or peanut oil
½ tablespoon ground dried crayfish

If using fresh spinach, cook, drain, and chop. Boil meat or fish in a little water until tender. Drain. Combine cayenne, tomato, and onion and cook in hot peanut oil until done. Stir in dried crayfish. Add chopped spinach and meat or fish and stir well. Simmer briefly to heat and blend flavors.

Makes 4 to 6 servings

**From: Best of Regional African Cooking
       (Nigeria)**

 # Cassava Foofoo

Peel 4 pounds cassava, wash, and soak in water 3 days. Drain and grate. Place in a clean sack and weight with something heavy so all the water is squeezed out. Let it remain weighted 3 days. When the cassava is quite dry, grind. Cover with a generous amount of cold water and strain. Leave in strainer overnight.

To cook, add enough cold water to the drained cassava to make into a thick, smooth paste which is not too soft. The amount of water required depends on how wet the cassava is to begin with. Put into an iron pot and stir over medium heat until cooked. When ready, the *foofoo* will be rather transparent and smooth.*

Serve as an accompaniment to soups.

*TIPS:

In some areas of Cameroon, *Cassava Foofoo* is steamed rather than boiled and is called *Miondo*.

**From: *Best of Regional African Cooking*
(Cameroon)**

85

 **Spinach Sauce**

Ingredients

2 onions, chopped
2 tablespoons oil
2 tomatoes, peeled and sliced
1 green pepper, chopped
2 pounds fresh spinach, chopped, or 2 (10-ounce)
    packages frozen chopped spinach, thawed
1 teaspoon salt
1 to 2 chili peppers or ½ to 1 tablespoon crushed
    red pepper
½ cup peanut butter

In a heavy sauce or stewing pan, sauté onions in hot oil until tender but not brown. Add tomatoes and green pepper and continue sautéing 1 or 2 minutes. Add spinach, salt, and chili peppers; cover and simmer 5 minutes. Mix peanut butter with a little water into a smooth paste and add to spinach. Stir well and continue cooking on a low heat about 10 minutes. Stir frequently. As no water is called for, a heavy pot and a low fire are essential to prevent scorching. You may, of course, add small amounts of water if you wish. Serve with a starch dish.

Makes 4 to 6 servings

**From: *Best of Regional African Cooking*
(Central African Republic)**

Groundnut-Squash Sauce

Ingredients

3 pounds zucchini or summer squash
½ pound unsalted peanuts, coarsely chopped
2 tablespoons oil

Cook the squash, whole and unpeeled, in a small amount of salted water until tender. Drain and mash. Mix with peanuts and oil in a saucepan and simmer 5 minutes to blend flavors. Sauce will be thick. Serve hot.

Makes 6 to 8 servings

From: ***Best of Regional African Cooking***
       (Chad)

 # Aubergine Baked in Coconut Cream

Ingredients

1 large eggplant
4 onions, finely chopped
1 teaspoon salt
¼ teaspoon dried chilies
1½ cups coconut cream
    (see recipe below)

for the **Coconut cream**
Fresh coconut meat
Water

To each tablespoon grated coconut add 1 tablespoon hot water. Stand for 30 minutes, then strain through muslin or cheese cloth to extract all the cream.

Variation
If using vacuum-packed flaked coconut, add 1 tablespoon hot, not boiling, double cream, instead of water.

Peel eggplant and slice thinly. Lay slices in a buttered shallow oven dish, spread with onions and sprinkle with salt and ground chilies. Pour coconut cream over. Cover closely and bake in a very moderate oven (350 degrees) for 45 minutes. Remove cover and bake for 5 to 6 minutes.

Makes 4 to 6 servings

From: ***Cooking the Caribbean Way***
(St. Maarten)

Bell Pepper with Onions, Tomatoes & Ginger

Ingredients

2 tablespoons corn oil
2 to 3 small pieces cinnamon stick
1 teaspoon black mustard seeds
1 teaspoon urad dal
1 onion, chopped lengthwise
1 tomato, chopped
½ tablespoon freshly ground or chopped ginger
½ teaspoon turmeric powder
1 teaspoon garam masala powder
1 teaspoon salt
2 bell peppers, chopped lengthwise
¼ cup plain yogurt

Heat corn oil with cinnamon stick in a cast-iron skillet over medium heat. When oil is hot, but not smoking, add mustard seeds and urad dal. Fry, covered, until mustard seeds burst (listen for popping sound) and urad dal is golden brown.

Add chopped onion, tomato and ginger. Stir fry for 1 minute over medium heat. Add turmeric powder, masala powder and salt. Mix well to obtain a thick paste-like consistency.

Add chopped bell peppers and blend well with sauce. Cover and reduce heat to low. Continue cooking until bell pepper is just tender, stirring occasionally. Be careful not to overcook!

Stir in the yogurt and mix well. Cook uncovered, over medium to low heat for 1 minute or so.

Makes 4 to 6 servings

From: *The Art of South Indian Cooking*

Asparagus Au Gratin
Asperges au gratin

Ingredients

18 asparagus stalks
1 teaspoon salt
1 tablespoon flour
1½ tablespoons butter
½ cup cream
½ cup broth
½ teaspoon grated nutmeg
¼ cup minced lean ham
2 tablespoons Parmesan cheese

Scrape the asparagus with care, cut into 1½-inch lengths—leave out the stalky ends—and cook in boiling water with salt until done.

Now place the asparagus in a baking dish, cover with the sauce, made with the flour, 1 tablespoon butter, cream, broth, and nutmeg, minced ham, grated cheese, and dot with the remaining ½ tablespoon butter. Brown in moderate oven (350 degrees) for about 20 minutes.

Makes 4 servings

From: *The Art of Dutch Cooking*

 # Creamed Spinach, with Cheese
Sabanikh Purée

Ingredients

1 pound spinach, chopped coarsely
1 tablespoon butter
½ cup milk
Salt
3 to 4 tablespoons grated Parmesan or hard,
      salted cheese
1 to 2 tablespoons bread crumbs

Wash and cook spinach, chop coarsely, and place in pot over flame with no water. Toss occasionally in closed pot and cook for about 10 minutes until spinach loses its moisture. Drain and whirl in a blender with butter, milk, salt, and 2 tablespoons cheese. Grease oven pan, sprinkle with bread crumbs, then pour in the spinach and top with the remaining cheese. Bake in center of preheated moderate oven.

Makes 4 to 6 servings

From: *Egyptian Cooking*

Baked Chayote
Choco

Chayote is known as *chocho* in the southern part of the Yucatan Peninsula, particularly in Belize. This recipe makes a rich casserole of brilliant colors. It is substantial enough to serve as a vegetarian main course or will blend well with almost any fowl, meat, or seafood entree.

To save time, the chayotes may be cooked early in the day or even the day before they will be needed. Once they have been simmered and cooled, the recipe is very easy to prepare and assemble.

Ingredients

3 large chayotes
Water as needed
½ teaspoon salt
2 tablespoons oil
1 onion, chopped
2 cloves garlic, diced
3 tomatoes, cut into eighths
1 green pepper, chopped
4 ounces grated Swiss cheese
4 ounces grated Muenster cheese

Place the chayotes in a saucepan with enough water to cover them. Add the salt and bring the water to a boil. Cover the pan and simmer the vegetables for about 1 hour, or until tender. Drain the chayotes and let them cool.

Peel the chayotes and cut them in half. Remove the seeds and any hard pithy parts. Cut each squash into ½-inch strips.

Preheat the oven to 375 degrees. Heat the oil in a heavy skillet. Sauté the onion until it is translucent. Add the garlic and sauté for 2 or 3 minutes more. Add the tomatoes and green pepper. Cook for another 5 minutes.

Transfer the vegetable mixture to a baking dish. Sprinkle the grated cheese on top, cover, and bake the chayote for 30 minutes. Remove the cover and bake for another 15 minutes, or until cheese is bubbly and golden-brown.

Makes 6 to 8 servings

From: ***Mayan Cooking: Recipes from the Sun***
      Kingdoms of Mexico
      (Belize)

 # Honey Baked Beans

"Every man to his taste" is an often repeated phrase and it seems that every man has his own notion about how baked beans should taste. This is one of many.

Ingredients

1 pound yellow eye-beans soaked overnight
Salt and baking soda
3 slices salt pork
2 tablespoons dry mustard
1 large onion, sliced
Water
1 to 2 cups maple syrup

Drain beans which have soaked overnight. Cover with fresh cold water, a little salt, and boil gently under cover until skin on beans splits when blown upon. To test, remove a bean or two from the pot with a spoon and blow. Keep testing until ready. Toss in several pinches of baking soda and stir. Continue cooking but take care not to overboil.

When the beans are really tender, drain in a colander. Partially dice a slice of salt pork and place in bottom of a bean pot or casserole which has a cover. Put in a layer, about ⅓ of the beans. Sprinkle with part of the dried mustard and onion slices. Put in another layer of beans and repeat until pot is full, slipping in a piece of salt pork here and there. Top with a larger piece of salt pork. Now pour in maple syrup. The quantity is dependent upon how sweet you like your beans. The liquid should be up to the top layer of beans so water should be added to the syrup to dilute it to the desired degree and keep the beans moist during the cooking process. It may be necessary to add more liquid during the baking. A little experimentation is necessary. The size and shape of the baking dish affects the quantity of liquid needed.

Bake in a slow oven (270 to 300 degrees) for at least 6 hours. Keep covered until time to brown the top. Turn up oven for a short time for this. It is strongly recommended that real maple syrup, not cane syrup, be used for the best results.

Makes 6 servings

**From: *Old Warsaw Cookbook*
(America)**

94

Swooned Priest
Mollah Ghash Kardeh

This dish is so delicious that even mulla is supposed to faint from the sheer joy of eating it!

Ingredients

2 large onions, sliced
3 large tomatoes, sliced
1 eggplant, peeled and sliced ½-inch thick
Salt and pepper
1 small bunch fresh coriander or parsley, minced
⅓ cup hot water
2 tablespoons oil
2 cloves garlic, sliced

95

Arrange onions, tomatoes, and eggplant in alternate layers in a frying pan, sprinkling over each layer with salt and pepper and the minced greens. Add water, oil, and garlic. Cover tightly and simmer for about 30 minutes or until the liquid is reduced to a rich gravy. Serve hot either with bread or *chelou, dami* or *kateh.*

Makes 4 servings

From: *The Art of Persian Cooking*

 ## Potato Pancakes
Placki Kartoflane

Ingredients

4 large potatoes, grated
1 large onion, minced
2 eggs
4 tablespoons sifted all-purpose flour
Salt
½ cup bacon drippings

Mix first five ingredients well. Heat bacon drippings in a heavy skillet until almost smoking. Drop batter by spoonfuls into skillet. Flatten each pancake with a fork. Fry until golden on both sides (do not crowd).

Makes 6 servings

From: *The Best of Polish Cooking*

 **Curry Cucumber**
(A Cape Dish)

Ingredients

4 large cucumbers (almost yellow)
1 pound mutton (fresh or cold), minced
1 slice bread, soaked in milk
1 egg
Salt and pepper
2 teaspoons curry powder, divided
2 large onions, sliced
1 tablespoon oil
1 teaspoon sugar
1 tablespoon vinegar
1 cup stock
1 tablespoon butter

Peel cucumbers carefully (be particular that no bitter be left). Take out the seeds, cut in halves across, or if large in three pieces. Combine the following: mutton, bread, egg, a little salt and pepper, and 1 teaspoon curry-powder. Mix well together, stuff the cucumber with this. Then fry onions, a nice brown in oil; make a paste of curry-powder, sugar, vinegar, stock, and butter; simmer in a flat stewing-pot. Arrange the stuffed cucumber in this, and let it simmer on a moderate heat for 2 hours.

TIPS:
Served with boiled rice, this is a nice *entrée* or lunch dish.

Makes 4 servings

From: *Traditional South African Cookery*

Eggplant Caviar

This is a favorite summer zakooska, made entirely with vegetable ingredients. It gets its name from the fact that we think it looks like caviar.

Ingredients

1 large eggplant
2 small onions, minced
4 tablespoons olive oil or
vegetable oil, divided
4 tablespoon tomato purée
2 teaspoons lemon juice
2 teaspoons salt
Freshly ground pepper

Drop the whole eggplant into a pot of boiling water. Cook about 25 minutes. Take out and let cool sufficiently to handle. Cut off the stem end; remove the skin; chop the eggplant *very* fine. Simmer the onion 10 minutes in a little of the oil, without browning. Add the chopped eggplant, the tomato purée, and 1 tablespoon of oil. Cook slowly for 15 minutes over gentle heat, uncovered, stirring from time to time. Continue cooking, gradually adding oil until quite thick. The cooking time depends on the eggplant, some being drier than others. About 1 hour should give the required consistency. Now add the lemon juice, salt, and a dash of freshly ground pepper.

For the oil, use at least 1 tablespoon olive oil to 3 of vegetable oil if possible. Olive oil improves the flavor.

Serve well-chilled.

Makes 6 servings

From: *The Best of Russian Cooking*

Mushroom Fricasse
Fricasse de Ciuperci

Ingredients

2 tablespoons butter, divided
2 teaspoons chopped scallions
2 garlic cloves, sliced
½ pound mushrooms*, diced, with stems
4 hard-boiled eggs
1 tablespoon chopped fennel
1 teaspoon salt
1 teaspoon black pepper
1 teaspoon crushed hot red pepper
2 teaspoons lemon juice
¼ cup beef stock
3 tablespoons sour cream
1 tablespoon all-purpose flour

In a skillet, heat 1 tablespoon butter over medium-high heat. Add scallions and garlic. Stir and sauté until scallions turn a light brown but do not burn, about 4 minutes. Add another tablespoon butter and mushrooms, stir and sauté another 4 to 5 minutes.

In the meantime, peel and slice hard-boiled eggs lengthwise. Arrange slices side by side to cover the bottom of serving plates, one egg per plate. To the mushrooms, add fennel, salt, pepper, red pepper, and lemon juice. Stir well. Add beef stock, cover, lower heat to low, and cook slowly until tender, about 10 minutes.

In a small bowl, mix sour cream with flour. Add mixture slowly to mushrooms, stirring well, and allow to simmer for another few minutes until the sauce thickens. Pour the mushroom sauce over the eggs, and serve.

TIPS:

Any mushrooms will do, but try to choose those with a strong flavor, such as shiitake, crimini, or cepes.

Makes 4 servings

From: *Taste of Romania*

 **Sauerkraut**

Ingredients

2 pounds sauerkraut
2 onions, sliced
2 slices bacon, diced
2 tablespoons butter
¼ teaspoon pepper
1 tablespoon caraway seeds
2 tablespoons sugar
½ cup beef bouillon
1 cup white wine

Rinse sauerkraut with warm water and drain well. Cook onion and bacon in butter until onion is soft. Add the drained kraut, pepper, caraway seeds, and sugar. Cover tightly. Cook 15 minutes. Add bouillon and wine. Simmer ½ hour longer. Serve with pork, poultry, or ham.

Makes 4 to 6 servings

**From: All Along the Danube
        (Slovak)**

Vegetable Pancake
Zeleninovy

Ingredients

3 egg whites
3 egg yolks
4 tablespoons melted butter
⅔ cup all-purpose flour
Salt and pepper
⅛ teaspoon mace
3 tablespoons milk
1½ cups chopped cooked vegetables (asparagus,
    cauliflower, peas and broccoli)
2 tablespoons butter
3 tablespoons all-purpose flour

Preheat oven to 350 degrees. Beat egg whites until stiff, then add 1 egg yolk at a time, blending well after each addition. Stirring constantly, slowly pour in the melted butter. Fold in flour and gently blend in the salt and pepper to taste, mace, milk, and vegetables. Butter an 8 x 8-inch baking pan well and dust it with flour. Fill pan with the batter and bake in preheated 350 degree oven for about 12 to 25 minutes until it is golden-brown. Cool. Slice into strips and use in soups or as a side dish with meat or fowl.

Makes 7 to 8 servings

From: ***All Along the Danube***
(Czech)

101

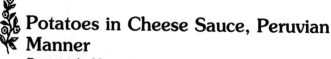

Potatoes in Cheese Sauce, Peruvian Manner
Papas á la Huancaina

Ingredients

½ pound cream cheese
4 hard-boiled egg yolks
1 teaspoon salt
¼ teaspoon dried ground chili peppers
½ cup olive oil
1 cup light cream
½ cup finely chopped onions
6 potatoes, cooked, cooled, and sliced
12 black olives

Cream the cheese with a wooden spoon, gradually working in the egg yolks. Mix in the salt and chili peppers. Beat in the oil, by the teaspoon, then the cream, and finally the onions. Pour over the potatoes and garnish with the olives.

Makes 6 to 8 servings

From: ***The Art of South American Cookery***
(Peru)

Meat Main Courses

Meat Loaf & Egg
El Belehat

Ingredients

1½ pounds ground beef
1 teaspoon cumin
1 teaspoon salt
½ teaspoon pepper
2 cloves garlic, crushed
4 eggs
3 tablespoons all-purpose flour
1 cup fresh bread crumbs
¼ cup olive oil
⅓ cup hot water
½ cup tomato juice

Combine ground beef with cumin, salt, pepper, and garlic, mix well. Hard-boil 2 of the eggs; peel but leave whole.

Sprinkle flour over a clean dish towel spread on a table. Flatten the meat out on the towel into a rectangle. Place the 2 hard-boiled eggs side-by-side near one edge and roll up the meat, jelly-roll fashion, so it looks like a large sausage. Press ends and edges together. Beat remaining eggs. Dip meat roll in the eggs, then roll in the bread crumbs.

Heat oil in a large frying pan. Brown the meat roll on all sides in the hot oil. Add hot water and tomato juice, cover, and simmer about 30 minutes or until done.

Serve hot or cold.

Makes 6 to 8 servings

From: Best of Regional African Cooking
(Egypt)

Algerian Couscous

Ingredients

2 pounds shoulder of lamb, cubed
1 large fryer chicken, including gizzard, cut into pieces
Olive oil
Salt and pepper
2½ pounds onions (preferably Spanish onions)
1 pound carrots, cut in pieces
1 pound leeks, cut in pieces
2 pounds medium or fine semolina (couscous)
Butter
1½ cups raisins
1½ pounds ground beef
1 clove garlic, chopped
1 egg
All-purpose flour
1 pound turnips, cut in pieces
1½ pounds zucchini, cut in pieces
1 pound green peppers, seeded and cut in pieces
1½ pounds tomatoes, peeled and cut in pieces
½ head cabbage, cut in pieces
2 (1-pound) cans chick peas, drained
1 or 2 chili peppers, ground
½ teaspoon cumin
½ teaspoon coriander
½ teaspoon chopped parsley
Pinch saffron
1 tablespoon lemon juice

Lacking a *couscous* cooker, you will need a heavy stewing pan or dutch oven deep enough to hold the meats and vegetables, plus a colander or steamer on top for steaming the semolina.

Brown the lamb and chicken pieces in a little olive oil; season with salt and pepper.

Put browned meats (with any remaining oil) into stewing pan with 1 onion, cut in pieces, carrots, and leeks. Cover with water, cover, and bring to a boil, and then reduce heat to simmer.

Take enough of the *couscous* to cover the bottom of the colander or steamer to a depth of about 1½ inches. Moisten lightly with cold, salted water, tossing the grains with the hands so all are moistened and the grains swell uniformly. Place the colander or steamer on top of the stewing pot, taking care the *couscous* does not come in contact with the cooking liquid. Seal edges by wrapping with a dampened, floured cloth so no steam escapes. (If the colander or steamer holes are too large to contain the *couscous*, wrap the *couscous* lightly in cheesecloth before placing in the colander.) Cover and let steam 35 to 40 minutes.

Meanwhile, mince remaining onions and sauté slowly in 4 tablespoons butter until they are soft. Salt lightly. Keep warm. Simmer raisins in 1 cup water about 30 minutes. Drain and keep warm. Season ground beef with salt and pepper. Mix with chopped garlic and egg. Form into small balls, dust lightly with flour, and brown well in butter. Keep hot.

Remove *couscous* from top of stewing pan (recover pan and continue simmering stew while proceeding with next steps). Wet *couscous* well with cold water, then drain. Stir through with a wooden spoon. Put in a bowl and add ½ cup water salted with 1 teaspoon salt. Work with hands, pulling apart and tossing lightly so the water penetrates each grain and the *couscous* swells. Repeat process with more salted water until semolina is well saturated. Set aside.

Cook remaining semolina as before, adding the first batch of semolina in 4 or 5 portions and mixing well after each addition.

When stew has been simmering 1 hour, add the turnips, zucchini, green peppers, tomatoes, cabbage, and chick peas.

When all the *couscous* has been cooked, the vegetables and meat should be tender (total cooking time for the *tajin* is between 1½ and 2 hours). Remove *couscous* from steamer and toss with ¼ pound butter, mixing lightly until butter is melted. Place *couscous* on a large dish, forming it into a mound. Make a good-sized well in the center. Place the chicken and lamb pieces in the well and surround with the sautéed onions. Sprinkle the raisins over all and arrange the meat balls on the *couscous*. Serve the vegetables with the cooking liquid, which has previously been reduced somewhat over a high fire, in a separate dish.

Pass with the *couscous* a sauce made of the chili peppers, cumin, coriander, parsley, and saffron mixed with ½ cup of the cooking liquid, 2 tablespoons olive oil, and 1 tablespoon lemon juice. This sauce is called *Harisa*. Without this hot pepper sauce, the Algerian *couscous* would be very pallid. It is available canned in some specialty food stores.

Makes 10 to 12 servings

From: **Best of Regional African Cooking
(Algeria)**

Barbecue Beef Skewers
Tsitsinga

Ingredients

1 pound round steak, cut in 1-inch cubes
2 cups salad oil
2 tablespoons vinegar
Salt
Tomatoes, peeled
Onions
Fresh ginger
3 chili peppers, or ½ to 1 tablespoon crushed red
      pepper, or ½ to 1 teaspoon cayenne
½ cup roasted corn flour

Marinate meat in a combination of ½ to 1 cup oil, the vinegar, and salt for at least 1 hour. Skewer meat and grill over charcoal until half done. Grind or blend enough tomatoes, onions, ginger, and peppers to make about 1 cup in all. (If using crushed red pepper or cayenne, add after grinding vegetables and ginger.) Remove meat from skewers and coat well with the vegetable mixture. Skewer meat again and roll in roasted corn flour. Dab generously with remaining oil and return to grill until done.

May be served cold with a salad for a light meal. As an entree, serve hot with rice.

Makes 4 to 6 servings

From: **Best of Regional African Cooking**
      (Ghana)

Beef in Groundnut Sauce

Ingredients

2 pounds beef or chicken
½ cup peanut oil, divided
1 pound soft tomatoes, peeled, seeded, and
    well-mashed
1 onion, finely chopped
1 teaspoon ground dried shrimp
½ to 1 teaspoon cayenne
Salt
1 cup peanut butter
2 cups water

Cut the meat into 2-inch cubes or the chicken into parts. Slowly brown in one-half the oil. Heat the remaining oil in a stewing pan; add mashed tomatoes, chopped onion, ground shrimp, cayenne, and salt to taste. Simmer about 15 minutes. Add browned meat or chicken. Dilute the peanut butter with the water and add to the meat mixture, mixing well. Cover and simmer over a moderately low fire until the meat is cooked, 20 minutes to 45 minutes depending on cut of beef used or size of chicken pieces. Serve with mashed yams.

Makes 6 servings

**From: *Best of Regional African Cooking*
        (Dahomey)**

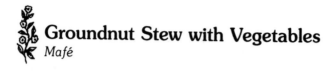

Groundnut Stew with Vegetables
Mafé

Ingredients

3 pounds beef, cut into 10 or 12 pieces (or 1 fryer
    chicken cut in pieces)
½ cup peanut oil
2 medium onions, finely chopped
1 pound plum tomatoes, peeled, seeded, and cut in half
2 cups water
Salt
Cayenne
2 green peppers, seeded and cut in pieces
½ pound acorn squash, peeled and diced
1 pound cassava root, diced (if available)
2 sweet potatoes, peeled and diced
1 turnip, diced
1 cup peanut butter
2 small eggplants, peeled and diced
1 head cabbage, cut in eighths

Brown the beef in the oil in a stewing pan. Remove meat and set aside. Sauté onions and tomatoes in the oil until onions are golden. Return meat and add water, salt, cayenne to taste, green peppers, squash, cassava root, sweet potatoes, and turnip. Cover and simmer 45 minutes. Mix peanut butter with about 1 cup of the cooking liquid into a smooth sauce. Add to pot with eggplants and cabbage. Cover and simmer 30 minutes more. Serve with boiled rice.

Makes 6 servings

From: ***Best of Regional African Cooking***
      (Senegal)

110

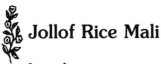

Jollof Rice Mali

Ingredients

1 pound tomatoes, peeled	2 cloves garlic, sliced
2 tablespoons tomato paste	1 chili pepper or
Peanut oil	½ teaspoon
2 large onions	cayenne
1 pound lamb, cut in	Salt and pepper
1-inch cubes	1 cup rice

Cut tomatoes into quarters and mash well with a fork. Add tomato paste.

Heat ¼ to ½ cup oil in a stewing pan. Mince 1 onion and brown. Add meat cubes and brown. Add mashed tomatoes and garlic.

Slice second onion, brush with oil, and broil until brown. Process broiled onions in blender with chili pepper or cayenne until ground. Add to meat mixture and season with salt and pepper. Add about 1 cup of water, stir well, and simmer over a low fire 45 minutes or until meta is tender.

Meanwhile, cook rice as directed on package until firm but not soft.

Serve with meat sauce poured over the rice.

Variation:

Other vegetables as available may be added to this dish. Peel and cut in pieces 3 carrots, 1 turnip, 1 large potato, and 1 small cabbage. Add along with the ground grilled onion mixture. If necessary, add a little more water.

Makes 4 servings

From: Best of Regional African Cooking
      (Mali)

111

 **Fresh Meat Stew**

Ingredients

1½ pounds beef, cut in cubes
2 cups water
3 onions, sliced
1 tomato, peeled and sliced
¼ to ½ cup peanut oil
2 chili peppers or ½ to 1 tablespoon crushed
     red pepper

In a heavy stewing pan, combine meat, water, and onions. Simmer 30 minutes. Add tomato, oil, and chili peppers. Continue simmering until meat is tender, 30 to 45 minutes more.

Variations:
This same stew may be made with chicken, lamb, or fish. Eliminate the chili pepper for a southern Zambian version. Both north and south in Zambia, this would be served with cornmeal mush, called *Nshima*.

Makes 4 to 6 servings

From: ***Best of Regional African Cooking***
       (Zambia)

Ethiopian Meat Stew

Ingredients

4 tablespoons butter or oil
1 large onion, chopped
1 cup water
1 pound boneless meat (beef, lamb, or veal) in
    1-inch cubes
½ teaspoon salt
¼ teaspoon each cayenne and pepper
½ tablespoon all-purpose flour
2 tablespoons cold water

In 2 tablespoons butter or oil, sauté onions over medium heat until soft. Add remaining butter or oil and water and simmer, uncovered, about 5 minutes. Add meat, salt, cayenne, and pepper. Simmer, covered, until meat is tender, 1 to 1½ hours. Blend flour and cold water and stir into stew. Cook over medium heat, stirring constantly, until stew liquid is thickened, about 5 minutes.

Makes 4 servings

From: ***Best of Regional African Cooking***
      (Ethiopia)

Spiced Barbecued Meat

Ingredients

4 small onions, very
    finely minced
2 cloves garlic, ground fine
1 teaspoon Cayenne
    pepper
1 tablespoon brown sugar
1 teaspoon fresh lime or
    lemon juice

1½ teaspoons curry powder
½ teaspoon ground cloves
½ teaspoon ground ginger
3 tablespoons water
1½ pounds steak, cubed
3 tablespoons melted butter
Peanut butter sauce

for the Peanut butter sauce
6 teaspoons prepared mustard
2 tablespoons peanut butter
1 teaspoon turmeric
2 tablespoons soy sauce
2 tablespoons Worcestershire sauce
Few drops Tabasco
Mix mustard into peanut butter, add remaining ingredients
and blend thoroughly.

Blend onions, garlic, Cayenne, sugar, juice and spices,
then add water. Put in meat and knead with the hands so that it
absorbs the liquid. Put in the refrigerator for 6 hours. Take 4 or
8 skewers, according to their length, thread cubes of meat on,
brush with melted butter. Put on a rack under the grill, about 3
inches from heat. Turn, brushing frequently with butter and cook
for 15 to 20 minutes, making sure all sides are exposed to heat.
Serve with peanut butter sauce.

Makes 4 servings

From: *Cooking the Caribbean Way*
      (Surinam)

Roast Leg of Lamb, á la Criolla

Ingredients

4 to 5 pound leg of lamb
1 clove garlic, chopped
¼ teaspoon black pepper
1 teaspoon oregano
1½ tablespoons olive oil
4 teaspoons salt
Extra pepper

Remove skin and excess fat from lamb and wipe meat with a damp cloth. Place on a rack in a shallow pan, fat side up. Carefully make superficial criss-cross cuts on top of the joint. Crush garlic, pepper and oregano together in a small bowl, using a wooden spoon. Add olive oil, salt and extra pepper and blend well. Rub into meat, cover and put in the refrigerator overnight.

Take out 30 minutes before required for cooking and drain off any liquid. Pour this back over the joint, then roast, uncovered, in a very moderate oven (350 degrees) allowing 35 to 40 minutes per pound. Use the pan drippings to make gravy.

Makes 6 to 8 servings

From: ***Cooking the Caribbean Way***
(Puerto Rico)

115

 **Lemon Lamb**

Ingredients

Juice of 4 limes or 2 lemons
2 tablespoons olive oil
2 tablespoons grated onion
1 tablespoon chili powder
2 teaspoons curry powder
2 teaspoons ground ginger
2 teaspoons turmeric
1 clove garlic, crushed
1 teaspoon salt
2 pound lamb, cut into 1½ inch cubes
4 onions, quartered
6 slices pineapple, halved
4 tomatoes, quartered
8 slices bacon, halved
1 green pepper

Combine juice, olive oil, grated onion, chili powder, curry powder, ginger, turmeric, garlic and salt. Blend well, then add lamb cubes and leave to marinate overnight in a cool place.

Put marinated meat on to long skewers alternating with pieces of onion, pineapple, tomato and bacon slices wrapped round pieces of green pepper. Place skewers on rack under the grill about 3 inches from the flame; grill for 15 to 20 minutes, turning often to brown all sides.

Serve with a dip of peanut butter sauce (see recipe for Spiced Barbecued Meat).

Makes 4 servings

From: Cooking the Caribbean Way
(Aruba)

Goat Meat Stew

Ingredients

3 pounds mutton, in 1-inch cubes
2 tablespoons butter
1 tablespoon tomato purée
1 large onion, chopped
3 cloves
1 clove garlic, crushed
1 tablespoon all-purpose flour
Salt
1 teaspoon pepper

Put meat, butter, tomato purée, onion, cloves, garlic, and most of the salt and pepper into a large saucepan; cover completely with cold water, bring to a boil and simmer for 2 hours. Mix flour with remaining salt and pepper, stir in enough water to make a thin paste. Stir this into the stew and cook until it thickens. Serve with rice and dasheen.*

*TIPS:
Dasheen looks like a turnip with broad green leaves; it is not essential if it does not grow around your way! Goat meat may be substituted for mutton and more pepper used for a stronger stew.

Makes 6 to 8 servings

From: *Cooking the Caribbean Way*
(Montserrat)

 # Wiener Schnitzel
Veal

Ingredients

4 veal escallopes (scaloppine)
All-purpose flour
1 egg, beaten
Cold milk
Salt
Bread crumbs
Oil (for frying)
Lemon wedges

Trim your Escallopes, make some incisions around the edge and beat them well. Prepare three deep plates; put some all-purpose flour in one; in the second, put a beaten egg with a little cold milk and a pinch of salt; and the third, fill with bread crumbs. Dip the Escallope first in flour, then shake it so that all the surplus comes off, dip it in the beaten egg, let this drip off, then finally into the bread crumbs. Do everything lightly and gently; do not press down the bread crumbs, just shake off the surplus.

Now into the frying pan. (Escallopes should be fried straight after the flour, egg, and bread crumb coating.) The fat must be smoking, it can be lard or oil, but it should be deep, and there must be plenty of room around each Schnitzel.

Lift out with a pastry slicer, so that the fat can drip off, and serve at once. Delicious with buttered parsley potatoes or rice and salad. A dash of cranberry sauce may be served to complement the Schnitzel. Don't forget to squeeze a wedge of lemon onto the meat.

TIPS:
Veal cutlets can be dealt with in the same way, also Escallopes of pork and pork chops.

Makes 4 servings

From: *The Best of Austrian Cuisine*

 Rio Grande Churrasco
(Churrasco á Rio Grande)

This recipe is for a large quantity of barbecue. You may use a variety of meats, such as beef tenderloin, some ribs of lamb, or even a whole lamb, cleaned and divided into large pieces, leg of lamb, ribs of beef or veal. The meat should be of the best quality, and tender.

Ingredients

10 to 15 pounds of meat
½ cup salt
3 cups hot water
6 cloves of garlic, finely mashed

Prepare your fire of charcoal or wood. For the genuine Rio Grande *churrasco*, it should be a wood fire. The coals should be bright before the meat is put on to roast. Spread the meat on the grill, but do not let the pieces touch. When the meat begins to brown, baste with the following: dissolve the salt in the hot water and add the garlic. Keep on basting until the meat is cooked. If you should run out of the basting liquid before the meat is cooked, prepare a little more. The meat should not be too close to the fire, or it may burn before it is cooked through. The garlic is optional, but even those who do not care for garlic

119

will find that it gives a delicate extra flavor. When the meat is done to your taste, leave it over the fire, which will have died down somewhat, and cut off pieces to serve. A tender rib cut at just the right stage of brownness and juiciness, eaten with the fingers, will never be forgotten.

Makes 15 to 20 servings

From: *The Art of Brazilian Cookery*

 Munich Cutlets

Ingredients

4 pork cutlets, very lean
Salt and pepper
Horseradish, grated (fresh or prepared)
All-purpose flour (to coat)
2 eggs, lightly beaten
Stale bread crumbs (to coat)
Oil (for frying)
Parsley leaves
Tomato slices
Lemon slices

Lightly flatten the cutlets, season them with salt and pepper, and coat them thickly with the horseradish. Dip them in flour to coat, and let them dry briefly before quickly dipping them in the eggs and subsequently coating them with the bread crumbs. In a frying pan, heat enough oil to cover the bottom well and fry the cutlets at medium heat on both sides until crisp. Garnish the cutlets with parsley leaves, tomato and lemon slices, and serve with a mixed salad.

Makes 4 servings

From: *Bavarian Cooking*

 # Finnish Hash
Pyttipannu

This is originally a Swedish dish and is a very popular way to use leftover beef and ham.

Ingredients

4 cups raw potatoes, peeled and cut into small cubes
2 tablespoons oil, divided
2 tablespoons butter, divided
2 medium onions, peeled and chopped
3 cups cooked beef or ham, or a combination of the two, cut into small cubes
Salt and pepper
4 to 6 eggs
1 tablespoon chopped parsley

After dicing the potatoes, keep them in cold water to prevent discoloration. Drain the potatoes and pat them dry in paper towels. Brown them over medium heat in half the butter and oil preferably in a nonstick skillet. Stir and shake the pan often to get them to brown evenly. When cooked, remove the potatoes to a dish and keep warm.

In the same skillet cook the onion in the rest of the butter and oil, until it is soft and lightly browned. Add the meats and brown them on all sides, stirring and shaking the pan to get an even result. Return the cooked potatoes into the pan and stir to mix well. Sprinkle with salt and pepper to taste. Transfer to a serving dish or individual plates and keep warm.

In the same skillet, cook the eggs only on one side, so that the yolk acts as a sauce for the hash. Serve the hash with the egg on top, sprinkled with parsley.

Makes 4 to 6 servings

From: *The Best of Finnish Cooking*

121

Dublin Coddle

This is a dish that is eaten by families who have lived for generations in Dublin and who look upon the city as their local village. Sean O'Casey ate Dublin coddle and Brendan Behan's mother still makes it. Dean Swift ate it in the Deanery of St. Patrick's Cathedral in the 18th century. It is eaten especially on Saturday night when the men come home from the pubs.

Ingredients

1 pound onions
6 slices bacon
1 pound sausages
Salt and pepper
1 cup water

Skin and slice the onions. Put them into a saucepan with the bacon and sausages. Season with salt and pepper to taste and add water. Lay wax paper on top. Cover with a tight lid and simmer gently for ½ hour.

This was always washed down by draughts of Irish stout.

Makes 6 servings

From: *The Art of Irish Cooking*

Veal Loaf Brussels Style
Pain de Veau

Ingredients

2 pounds ground veal
2 pounds ground pork
¼ cup finely chopped onion
1 tablespoon finely chopped parsley
½ cup bread crumbs
1 tablespoon heavy cream or evaporated milk
2 eggs
2 tablespoons salt
¼ teaspoon pepper
⅛ teaspoon nutmeg
2 tablespoons all-purpose flour
½ stick butter
½ cup white wine

Mix in a deep dish the veal, pork, onion, parsley, bread crumbs, cream and eggs. Add salt, pepper and nutmeg to taste.

Mold into loaf. Roll in flour. Butter the bottom of an oven-proof baking dish and place the veal loaf in it. Cover with dabs of butter. Bake in hot oven (475 degrees) for 1½ hours.

A few minutes before it is done, pour wine over the veal loaf and mix into the pan drippings.

Makes 6 servings

From: *A Belgian Cookbook*

Pomegranate Khoreshe
Khoreshe Anar

Ingredients

1 pound fresh coriander leaves or parsley
1 ounce mint leaves
6 tablespoons oil, divided
1 pound ground meat
1 onion, minced
½ teaspoon pepper
1 teaspoon salt
½ teaspoon turmeric
½ teaspoon ground clove (optional)
8 ounces coarsely chopped walnut
2 cups pomegranate juice

Mince the coriander or parsley and the mint leaves and sauté them in 3 tablespoons hot oil until wilted. Mix meat, onion, pepper, salt, turmeric, and clove and form tiny meat balls. Sauté in the remaining oil with onion until browned on all sides. Add to the vegetables. Add walnuts and pomegranate juice and simmer, partially covered, about 1 hour, or until a rich gravy rises to the top.

Makes 4 servings

From: *The Art of Persian Cooking*

Homemade Kielbasa
Kielbasa Domowa

Ingredients

3 pounds raw pork shoulder, chopped, or
    coarsely ground
¾ pound raw beef chuck, coarsely ground
1 tablespoon salt
½ teaspoon pepper
¼ teaspoon marjoram
3 cloves garlic, chopped
2 teaspoons honey
Sausage casings

Combine all the ingredients except casings, and mix well. Sauté until well done and stuff into casings, forming foot-long links. Refrigerate for 4 days to cure.

Makes 8 servings

From: *The Best of Polish Cooking*

Caraway Pork Chops & Apples

Ingredients

6 pork chops, ½-inch thick
Salt
Pepper
Powdered sage
2 tablespoons butter
9 apples, halved and cored
1 teaspoon caraway seeds

Sprinkle pork chops with salt, pepper, and sage to taste. In a frying pan, quickly brown chops on both sides in melted butter. Arrange 12 of the apple halves, slightly overlapping, cut side up, in bottom of greased baking dish (about 9 × 13-inch). Sprinkle apples with caraway seeds. Arrange browned chops in a single layer over apples. Prick remaining apple halves with fork. Top each chop with one apple half, placed cut side down. Scrape drippings from frying pan and pour over apples and chops. Cover pan and bake in moderately hot oven (375 degrees) for 25 minutes. Twice during baking, remove cover and baste apples with juice in bottom of baking dish. Remove cover and bake 10 minutes more or until apples and chops are tender.

Makes 6 servings

From: *The Best of Scandinavian Cooking*

 **Sheep's Haggis**

Ingredients

The stomach-bag of a sheep
The pluck—*i.e.* the heart, liver, and lights
½ pound minced beef-suet
4 onions (parboiled)
2 teacupfuls toasted oatmeal
Pepper and salt
2 cups of the pluck boilings

Wash the bag well in cold water, put it into hot water, and scrape it; then let it lie in cold water all night with a little salt. Wash the pluck well; put it into a pan, letting the windpipe hang over the side; cover it with boiling water, add a teaspoon of salt, and let it boil for 2 hours; then take it out of the pan, and when it is cold cut away the windpipe. Grate ¼ of the liver (not using the rest for the haggis), and mince the heart and lights, the suet and the parboiled onions.

Add to all these the oatmeal, which has been dried and toasted to a golden color before the fire or in the oven; also the pepper and salt, and 1 pint of the liquor in which the pluck was boiled. Mix these all well together. Take the bag and fill it little more than half full of the mince; if it is too full, it will burst in boiling. Sew up the hole with needle and thread, and put the haggis into a pan of boiling water. Prick the bag occasionally with a needle, to prevent it bursting. Boil this for 3 hours, then serve it on a hot plate.

Makes 6 servings

From: *Traditional Food from Scotland*

 **Beef Stroganoff**

Ingredients

1½ pounds fillet of beef or lean part of the tenderloin
1½ teaspoons salt
2 teaspoons pepper
3 tablespoons butter, divided
1 tablespoon all-purpose flour
1 cup consommé
1 scant teaspoon prepared hot mustard
1 onion, sliced
3 tablespoons thick sour cream

There are several modified variations of Beef Stroganoff, but this is the classic Russian recipe. The secret of the sauce is the mustard.

Remove all fat and gristle from the meat. Cut it in narrow strips about 2 inches long and ½-inch thick. Dust the strips of beef with the salt and pepper, then set them aside for 2 hours. Do not put them in a cold place.

Melt 1½ tablespoons of the butter and blend in the flour. Add the consommé and boil. Stir in the mustard.

In another pan brown the strips of meat very quickly with the sliced onion in the remaining 1½ tablespoons butter.

Have the sour cream at room temperature. Add it to the mustard sauce and boil up once, then add the meat to the sauce. Don't put the onion in. Cover the pan and keep hot for 20 minutes, taking care it doesn't boil or even simmer. Set the pan over brisk heat for 3 minutes just before serving. Serve immediately.

TIPS:
Even this classic recipe for Beef Stroganoff has undergone local

changes during the past 20 years. Through the south of Russia 1 tablespoon of tomato purée has crept into the sauce. Or a few cooked mushrooms, sliced, may be introduced. In America the tomato purée and the mushrooms are both added. There have been ultra-conservative Russian gourmets who even prefer to leave the mustard out of the sauce; they substitute a few drops of lemon juice. Others permit a few drops of strong mushroom ketchup, which is termed "mushroom essence" in Russia. The result may, indeed, be tasty. . . . But it *isn't* Beef Stroganoff.

Makes 6 servings

From: *The Best of Russian Cooking*

Leg of Lamb
Gigot á la Provençale

Ingredients

5 to 6 pound leg of lamb
4 slices of bread
1 cup milk
7 slices bacon, chopped
Salt and pepper
Thyme
Parsley, chopped
3 cloves garlic, chopped
2 eggs
Onions, quartered
Carrots, chopped in 1 to 2-inch pieces
1 cup white wine

Bone your leg of lamb. Soak the bread in milk and squeeze dry. Mix with chopped bacon (smoked lard would taste even better). Season with salt and pepper, and add thyme, parsley, chopped garlic and eggs. Stuff the roast and sew up the cavity with a heavy thread. Place in a moderate oven with onions and carrots. Add wine and some water. Baste occasionally. In 2 hours, your leg of lamb should be tender. Serve with French fries and eggplant.

Makes 6 servings

From: ***Old Warsaw Cookbook***
(France)

 Sauerbraten

Ingredients

3 to 4 pounds chuck beef roast
3 cloves garlic, sliced
Sage
Thyme
Rosemary
Salt and pepper
5 cups water
1 lemon, sliced
2 cups wine vinegar
2 large onions, sliced
1 tablespoon sugar

With a sharp, pointed knife prepare slits in your roast, and insert pieces of garlic and spices. Rub with salt and pepper and place in an earthenware bowl. Bring to a boil water, slices of lemon, vinegar and pour it over the meat (top the meat with slices of onion). Cover and let stand for 2 days. Cook in the oven, under cover for 2 hours. Add the sugar to the meat sauce. Serve with boiled potatoes.

Makes 6 servings

**From: Old Warsaw Cookbook
(Germany)**

 # Isle of Man Hot Pot

Ingredients

Large neck of mutton
1 pound onions, chopped in 1-inch pieces
2 pounds potatoes, cubed
½ pound leeks, chopped
½ pound carrots, chopped in 1-inch pieces
Seasonings
Water (to cover)

Place meat on base of large pot. Cover over and around with the onions, potatoes, leeks, and carrots. Season and cover with water. Simmer gently for 3 to 3½ hours.

Makes 6 to 8 servings

From: *Celtic Cookbook*

Bratwurst and Sauerkraut

Ingredients

1 pound beef sausage
½ pound sauerkraut
¼ pound mushrooms
2 tablespoons butter
½ small onion, sliced
Salt and pepper
1 tablespoon sugar
1 cup brown sauce (see below)

for the **Brown Sauce**

4 tablespoons bone marrow
1 onion, chopped
2 tablespoons all-purpose flour
1 cup meat stock
Parsley, chopped
Thyme
Sage
1 clove garlic
Salt and pepper
1 cup white wine

Melt marrow bone. Brown onion, add flour, stir constantly until browned. Add hot meat stock gradually and mix. Add parsley, thyme, sage, garlic, and salt and pepper. Then add the wine. Simmer together for a few moments.

Broil the sausage. Place the sauerkraut in an oven proof dish. Add sausage. Slice mushrooms and sauté lightly with onion. Top the sausage and sauerkraut. Sprinkle with sugar. Cover with brown sauce, and put in the oven for 15 minutes.

Makes 4 to 6 servings

**From: Old Warsaw Cookbook
(Germany)**

133

Boiled Beef Baked in Horseradish Sauce

Ingredients

¼ cup all-purpose flour
3 tablespoons butter
1 cup stock (from meat)
4 tablespoons horseradish
¾ teaspoon sugar
½ cup sour cream and 2 egg yolks
1 beef roast (3 to 4 pounds)

for the Horseradish sauce

Lightly brown flour in butter, thin this down with a cup of broth (in which the meat has been cooked), adding horseradish. Horseradish preserved in vinegar may also be used, but then the amount of lemon juice added to the sauce should be smaller. Add also sugar. Cook this sauce for 5 minutes and when it thickens add sour cream blended with 2 raw egg yolks. Heat the sauce for a moment, mixing it and not allowing it to boil. Pour the hot sauce over the meat.

This sauce may also be used for boiled ox tongue, which is then baked. In that case tongue stock is used instead of broth. This manner of serving boiled meat (and tongue) is very popular in Polish cookery.

Cut into thin slices meat cooked in broth, after letting it cool. Arrange the meat on a dish (a shallow oval flame-proof casserole is best) and, having garnished it with the diced vegetables from the broth (this is not necessary), pour over horseradish sauce so that each slice of meat is covered, sprinkle with a teaspoon of butter and bake briefly in the oven until the surface of the sauce browns lightly.

Serve with mashed potatoes with pickles that are peeled and cut into quarters length-wise. Small freshly salted pickles may be served whole.

Makes 4 servings

From: *Old Polish Traditions in Kitchen & Table*

Polish Hunter's Stew
Bigos

Bigos is a composition not only complex, but also with a great many variants. In each Old Polish kitchen it was made in a different way, in accordance with home traditions. Thus, there was hunting *bigos*, Lithuanian *bigos*, rascal's *bigos* and others, made with sauerkraut, and fresh cabbage only. The addition of roast game raises the flavour of *bigos* considerably, but without game it will be just as excellent. Sauces from roast meats are also added to the *bigos*. Cook the *bigos* in an enameled or cast-iron enameled pot, but never in an aluminum one.

Ingredients

1½ pounds sauerkraut
1½ pounds fresh cabbage
4 large sour apples, peeled and finely chopped
2 ounces dried mushrooms
1 cup beef stock
2 large onions, finely chopped and lightly browned
     in butter
20 prunes, stones removed and sliced into strips
Salt
Pepper
Sugar
½ to ⅔ cup dry red wine or madeira
2 pounds various meats (pork roast, roast beef, joint
     of pork, roast duck, kielbasa), cubed

For final re-heating:
All-purpose flour
Butter
1 tablespoon tomato paste

The sauerkraut can be chopped and the fresh cabbage can be thinly sliced and scalded with boiling water before cooking. Cook the cabbage over low heat in a small amount of water (better: in the stock from cooked kielbasa). Add apples to the cabbage and sauerkraut mixture. Separately, cook at least 2 ounces dried mushrooms. Slice the cooked mushrooms thinly and add to the cabbage and heat along with the stock.

Now add browned onions. While the *bigos* is simmering, add the 20 prunes (stoned), cut into strips. (The prunes may be substituted by 1 to 2 tablespoons well-fried plum butter.) Season the *bigos* with salt, pepper and, if desired, with a little sugar. It should be sharp in taste. Finally, add dry red wine or madeira and the meats. After adding all the ingredients, cook the *bigos* over low heat for 40 minutes (careful: stir often, as it tends to burn). Cool to room temperature and refrigerate overnight. Next day, reheat the *bigos* over low heat for 2 to 3 hours. Add a little water or stock if necessary. Cool and refrigerate overnight again. It is tastiest and "mature" after the third reheating.

For final re-heating: Some add a roux of all-purpose flour lightly browned in butter, which makes the *bigos* thicker. But if the *bigos* is well-cooked, this addition is unnecessary.

The *bigos* may also be seasoned with tomato paste. Old Polish cuisine did not make use of this because it was not known then. But the addition of tomato paste is recommended.

Serve it very hot. Whole-wheat (or white) bread is served separately, along with a glass of chilled vodka (Wyborowa, Rye or Zubrówka), which improves digestion.

Makes 6 to 8 servings

From: *Old Polish Traditions in Kitchen & Table*

Eggplant Kebab
Yalanci Dolma

Ingredients

1½ pounds boneless, fat-free cubed lamb, veal, or beef,
    trimmed of fat and cubed
2 medium onions, chopped
4 tablespoons butter, divided
3 medium tomatoes (2 diced, 1 sliced)
Salt and pepper
4 medium eggplants
2 green peppers, seeded and cut into rings

In a saucepan sauté the meat and onions in 1 tablespoon butter, stirring occasionally until meat is browned, about 10 minutes. Add the diced tomatoes, salt, and pepper, cover, and cook over low heat until meat is tender.

Cut the stem off the eggplants. Then peel off ½-inch wide strip of the black skin lengthwise leaving the next ½-inch with the skin on. Repeat until you make a striped effect. Then cut vegetable crosswise into 1-inch thick round slices. Place slices in a deep tray and salt them generously. Fill tray with cold water. Leave about 30 minutes. Squeeze out the bitter juice, wash with cold water and dry.

Place 3 tablespoons butter in a frying pan. Heat and sauté eggplant slices on both sides. Place in a shallow flat cooking pot in one layer. Spread the cooked meat on top. Garnish with green pepper rings and tomato slices.

Cover and cook over a medium heat for about 20 to 25 minutes. Serve hot.

Makes 4 to 6 servings

From: *The Art of Turkish Cooking*

Swedish Meatballs No. 1
Köttbullar

Ingredients

1 pound roundsteak
½ pound lean pork
½ cup chopped onions
½ cup bread crumbs, or 1 cup raw grated potatoes
2 cups milk or water
2 egg-yolks, 1 white
Salt and pepper
Oil or butter (for frying)

Grind beef and pork 2 or 3 times together. Sauté onions and mix with meat, bread crumbs (or potatoes), milk (or water), egg-yolks and white, and salt and pepper to taste. Work mixture 15 minutes. Put in refrigerator for at least 2 hours. Roll into balls—fry in hot oil or butter, browning balls all around. Deep frying makes them brown outside, and tasty and moist inside. Serve with or without brown gravy made of stock.

Makes 30 meatballs

From: *The Best of Smorgasbord Cooking*

Swedish Meatballs No. 2
Köttbullar

Ingredients

½ loaf white bread
2 cups milk
1 pound round steak
1 pound veal
1 pound fresh pork
1 cup grated onions
1 cup grated raw potatoes
2 cups beer
1 tablespoon sugar
1 tablespoon salt (or more)
½ teaspoon pepper
Oil, fat, or butter, or mixed (for frying)
Evaporated milk (for gravy)

Cut crust from bread and soak in milk 1 hour. Grind meat 2 or 3 times with onions and potatoes. Mix with beer, sugar, salt, and pepper. Add more seasoning if necessary. Make medium sized balls and fry in deep fat or frying pan. Make gravy from stock and part evaporated milk, or serve meatballs plain with brown beans.

Makes 50 meatballs

From: *The Best of Smorgasbord Cooking*

Devon Breakfast Dish: Lamb's Fry

Ingredients

Lamb's fry
A little all-purpose
    flour
Salt and pepper
1 small onion
½ stick butter
1 lemon
A little parsley

Wash and dry the fry, cut it up in small slices, and roll it in a little flour seasoned with salt and pepper. Chop the onion finely, and cook it in the butter until light brown, then add the lamb's fry and cook gently for about 10 minutes, until it is well-browned. Add a squeeze of lemon juice when it is dished, sprinkle some finely chopped parsley and serve very hot.

Makes 4 to 6 servings

From: ***Traditional Food from England***

Little Grilled Sausages
Mititei (The Wee Ones)

Mititei have been associated with Romanian cuisine since 1865–1866. In Bucharest on Covaci Street, a popular inn named La Iordachi (At Iordachi's) was well-known for its delicious sausages. One night, so the story goes, the kitchen ran out of one kind of beef sausage, so they mixed the ingredients left over, rolled them into small sausage-shaped patties, and grilled them on charcoal without the usual casing. Regular customers loved them so much that they asked for more of "the wee ones without skin," and with time they became known as *mititei*, or "the wee ones."

Ingredients

2 pounds medium-lean ground beef*
2 tablespoons olive oil
2 tablespoons water
3 garlic cloves, crushed
2 teaspoons bicarbonate of soda
½ teaspoon dried thyme
½ teaspoon crushed hot red pepper
½ teaspoon hot Hungarian paprika
1 teaspoon caraway seeds
2 teaspoons salt
1 teaspoon fresh ground black pepper

Place ground beef in a bowl, and add all the ingredients in the order listed. Mix well and then knead mixture with your hands for not less than 5 minutes, wetting your hands frequently. This is important because the water from your hands mixes with the meat and helps keep the *mititei* moist. Place mixture in a bowl, cover with a plate or foil, and refrigerate at least 5 hours or overnight.

By tablespoonfuls, with damp hands, make small meatballs. Then roll between your hands into sausages about 3" long and 1" thick.

Grill or barbecue, turning *mititei* frequently to cook evenly**.
Tips:
Mititei can also be made from ground lamb, mutton, pork, or a combination of meats.

**Use tongs, not a fork, to turn the *mititei*, so as not to pierce them. This will keep the juices in the meat.

Makes 4 servings

From: **Taste of Romania**

Greek Lasagna (Pasticio) & Béchamel Sauce

Ingredients

1 tablespoon salt
1 package pasticio pasta (or ziti or penne pasta)
½ cup margarine
3 egg whites
2½ cups grated kefalotyri cheese, divided
¼ cup olive oil plus additional for pan
1 large onion, grated
3 cloves garlic, crushed
1 tablespoon fresh chopped mint
1 tablespoon fresh chopped basil
2½ pounds lean ground beef or lamb
½ cup white wine
1 can (16 ounces) crushed tomatoes
1 stick cinnamon
2 whole cloves
Salt and pepper
¼ cup dried bread crumbs
Béchamel sauce (see recipe below)

for the Béchamel Sauce

Béchamel sauce is used for mousaka, pasticio and other dishes.

2 sticks butter
1 cup all-purpose flour
6 cups hot milk
5 large eggs
½ cup kefalotyri cheese or grated romano cheese
Salt and pepper
½ teaspoon nutmeg

In a medium saucepan, melt the butter and gradually add the flour. Continue stirring for 3 to 4 minutes, adding hot milk and keep stirring for a smooth and creamy consistency. Remove saucepan from the heat.

In a blender, beat the eggs and cheese. With the blender on, slowly add 1 cup of the hot mixture to eggs and beat well for 2 to 3 minutes. Return egg mixture to saucepan and add salt and pepper and nutmeg, stirring constantly. Simmer until mixture is thick and smooth.

Yields 6 to 7 cups

Preheat the oven to 350 degrees. Fill a large pot with water. Add the salt and bring to a boil. Add the pasta and boil for only 15 minutes. Drain and put pasta into a large bowl. Melt the margarine in a small pan and pour it over the pasta. Lightly beat the egg whites and pour over the pasta. Using your hands, blend together the pasta and egg whites plus ¾ cup of the cheese.

Put the oil into a medium pan and add the onion, garlic, mint, and basil. Sauté until tender. Add the ground meat and sauté lightly. Stir constantly to break up all the lumps. Slowly add the wine, crushed tomatoes with juice and ½ cup of water. Add the cinnamon, cloves, salt and pepper to taste. Simmer for 20 minutes or until most of the water has evaporated. Take the pan off the stove and mix in ½ cup cheese and the breadcrumbs. Remove the cinnamon stick and cloves and stir the mixture well.

Prepare the béchamel sauce. Butter a baking pan, 10 × 15 × 2½-inches, and sprinkle the bottom with half of the remaining cheese. Arrange half of the pasta mixture in the pan. Spread the meat mixture on top of the pasta. Arrange the remaining pasta on top of the ground meat in the same direction as before. Pour the béchamel sauce over the top layer of pasta and sprinkle it with rest of cheese. Bake for 1 hour. As soon as the top is golden-brown, remove. Let it cool before cutting.

TIPS:
Pasticio macaroni may be purchased at any Greek market.

Makes 8 servings

From: *Best of Greek Cuisine: Cooking With Georgia*

Mousaka
(Mousakas)

Ingredients

4 large eggplants
1 cup vegetable oil (for frying)
¼ cup olive oil
1 large onion, finely chopped
3 cloves garlic, finely chopped
¼ cup finely chopped fresh parsley
2 tablespoons fresh chopped mint
2 tablespoons finely chopped fresh basil
2 ½ pounds ground lamb or beef
¼ cup white wine
1 teaspoon ground cinnamon
Salt and pepper
1 (16 ounce) can crushed tomatoes
¼ cup dried bread crumbs
½ cup grated kefalotyri cheese, divided
Béchamel sauce (see previous recipe)

Preheat oven to 350 degrees. Peel and wash the eggplants. Slice them lengthwise into 1 inch slices. Put the eggplants into a large bowl with enough water to cover. Add 1 tablespoon of salt, then let them sit in it for 1 hour to rid them of bitterness. Remove eggplants and place on paper towels and pat dry. In a large skillet, heat the vegetable oil and fry the eggplants on both sides until light brown. Drain on paper towels and set aside. Heat the olive oil in a medium pot. Add the onion, garlic, parsley, mint and basil. Sauté for 5 minutes. Add the ground meat and sauté until barely brown. Add the wine while continuously stirring to break up any lumps. Add cinnamon, salt and pepper to taste, and crushed tomatoes with juice. Cover the pot and simmer over medium heat for 25 to 30 minutes.

Remove from the stove and let cool for 5 minutes. Add bread crumbs and ¼ cup kefalotyri cheese to the meat sauce and mix it well. Arrange half of the eggplants on the bottom of a 10 × 15-inch baking pan, sprinkle with ¼ cup of the cheese and cover the eggplants with an even layer of the meat mixture. Layer the remaining eggplants on top of the meat mixture. Spread the béchamel sauce over the eggplants and sprinkle the top with the remaining cheese. Bake for 1 hour or until the top is a golden-brown. Remove from the oven and let cool for 20 minutes before cutting.

Makes 8 servings

From: *Best of Greek Cuisine: Cooking With Georgia*

Rabbit Casserole with Olives
Guiso de Conejo con Aceitunas

Ingredients

4 cups water
3 teaspoons vinegar
1 young rabbit (about 2½ pounds), cut into pieces
All-purpose flour (for dredging)
1 tablespoon lard
2 medium onions, chopped
1 bay leaf
2 cloves garlic, chopped
2 cloves
1 cup red wine
¾ cup white stock
Seasoning
1 tablespoon ground blanched almonds
Small jar (3 ounces) pitted green olives, halved
1½ cups (about 6 ounces) button mushrooms
1 tablespoon chopped green coriander

Put the water and vinegar into a large dish, add the rabbit pieces and allow to marinate overnight. Then remove and dry on a paper towel.

Dredge the rabbit pieces in seasoned flour.

Heat the oil and lard in a large, heavy casserole and lightly brown the rabbit all over. Remove the rabbit and add the chopped onions, bay leaf and garlic to the fat in the pan and sauté until soft.

Add the cloves, wine, stock and seasoning to taste. Mix well, cover and allow to simmer gently for about 1 hour.

About 15 minutes before serving, remove the lid, stir in the ground almonds, olives and mushrooms and allow the sauce to thicken.

Serve with rice and garnish with coriander.

Makes 4 servings

From: *A Spanish Family Cookbook*

 # Pot Roast Dubrovnik Style

Ingredients

4 to 5 pounds brisket, top round, or chuck
½ cup flour
Salt and pepper to taste
¼ cup olive oil, or any other oil
1 large onion, thinly sliced
2 to 3 cloves mashed garlic
5 scraped carrots, thinly sliced into circles
4 tomatoes, chopped
1 cup tomato sauce
1 cup chopped parsley
½ cup dry red wine
3 tablespoons chopped capers
¼ cup chopped green olives
6 to 8 thin slices of Provolone or Fontina cheese
½ pound pasta shells
3 tablespoons butter

For this recipe, you may use almost any cut of meat, but brisket is the best. Dredge the meat thoroughly in flour and sprinkle it with salt and pepper. Heat oil in a large pot or Dutch oven, add meat, and brown it on both sides. Add onion and garlic, reduce heat, and cook for 35 minutes, turning meat often. Add carrots and seasoning and cook ½ hour longer. Add tomatoes, tomato sauce, and parsley. Cook for 1½ hours, or until meat is very tender. Add wine, capers and green olives and cook for 15 minutes. Place thinly sliced cheese on top of meat, cover, and simmer until cheese is melted. Remove the meat to a heated platter and keep warm.

Cook pasta shells as directed on the package, drain well, add 3 tablespoons of butter, place the shells into the sauce, and bring to a boil. Remove from heat. Surround thinly sliced meat with shells and sauce. Serve Parmesan cheese on the side.

Makes 6 to 8 servings

From: **All Along the Danube**
(Croatia)

 ## Steak & Onions
Biftec con Cebollas

Ingredients

1 stick butter, divided
3 cups finely chopped onions
1½ teaspoons salt
½ teaspoon freshly ground black pepper
4 fillets of beef or individual steaks

Melt all but 2 tablespoons butter in a skillet; sauté the onions over very low heat for 30 minutes, but do not let them brown. Season with the salt and pepper; remove from skillet and keep warm. Melt the remaining butter in the same skillet; cook the steaks in it to desired degree of rareness. Transfer to a serving dish and spoon the onions over them.

Makes 4 servings

From: **The Art of South American Cookery**
(Uruguay)

Braised Steak With Peanut-Butter Sauce

Ingredients

3 pounds round steak
1½ teaspoons salt
½ teaspoon freshly ground black pepper
2 teaspoons Spanish paprika
4 tablespoons olive oil, divided
1 cup chopped onions
½ cup chopped green peppers
1½ cups peeled chopped tomatoes
6 tablespoons peanut butter
2 cups milk, scalded
6 potatoes, cooked and sliced
2 tablespoons minced parsley
2 hard-boiled eggs, chopped

Buy the steak in 1 piece. Season with the salt, pepper, and paprika. Heat 2 tablespoons oil in a casserole; brown the steak in it. Cover and cook over very low heat 1½ hours, or until tender. Add a little water if necessary, to keep from burning.

Prepare the sauce while the steak is cooking. Heat the remaining oil in a skillet; sauté the onions and green peppers for 10 minutes. Add the tomatoes; cook over low heat for 20 minutes. Stir in the peanut butter, and gradually add the milk, stirring steadily until thickened. Taste for seasoning. Cover the steak with the potatoes and pour sauce over all. Sprinkle with the parsley and eggs.

Makes 6 to 8 servings

From: *The Art of South American Cookery*
(Argentina)

151

Peruvian Skewered BBQ Meat
Anticuchos

Ingredients

1 beef heart or 2 pounds sirloin steak
1½ teaspoons salt
½ teaspoon dried ground chili peppers
6 peppercorns
¼ teaspoon saffron
3 cloves garlic, minced
1 cup tarragon vinegar
½ cup water
¼ cup olive oil

Beef heart is used in Peru when preparing *Anticuchos*, but steak is a good substitute. Wash the heart, remove the skin, and cut in 1-inch cubes, or cut the steak in 1-inch cubes. In a bowl, mix the salt, chili peppers, peppercorns, saffron, garlic, vinegar, and water. Marinate the meat in the mixture overnight in the refrigerator.

Drain the meat (reserving the marinade) and thread on 4 to 6 skewers. Brush with the olive oil. Broil as close to the heat as possible until heart is tender, or steak is at desired degree of rareness. Turn skewers frequently and baste with the marinade.

Makes 4 to 6 servings

From: The Art of South American Cookery
   (Peru)

Mixed-Meat Hash
Picadillo

Ingredients

¼ cup olive oil
1 cup chopped green peppers
1 cup chopped onions
1 clove garlic, minced
1 pound ground beef
½ pound ground pork
1½ teaspoons salt
½ teaspoon freshly ground black pepper
½ cup canned tomato sauce
¼ cup dry white wine
½ cup seedless raisins
¼ cup capers
½ cup sliced almonds

Heat the oil in a large skillet; sauté the green peppers, onions and garlic for 5 minutes. Add the beef and pork; cook over medium heat, stirring constantly until browned. Mix in the salt, pepper, tomato sauce, wine and raisins. Cook on low heat for 25 minutes, mixing frequently. Add the capers and almonds; cook 5 minutes longer.

Makes 4 to 6 servings

**From: *The Art of South American Cookery*
(Ecuador)**

Bolivian Pork Casserole
Ají de Puerco

Ingredients

½ cup olive oil
3 cups chopped onions
2 cloves garlic, minced
3 pounds pork, cut in _-inch squares
4 tablespoons raw rice
1½ cups chopped tomatoes
2 cups beef broth
2 teaspoons salt
½ teaspoon freshly ground black pepper
¼ teaspoon dried ground chili peppers
¼ teaspoon saffron
4 potatoes, peeled and quartered
3 firm bananas, cut in 2-inch lengths
½ cup ground peanuts
½ cup heavy cream
1 tablespoon molasses

Heat the oil in a casserole; sauté the onions for 5 minutes. Mix in the garlic and pork until browned. Add the rice and tomatoes; cook for 10 minutes. Stir in the broth, salt, pepper, chili peppers and saffron. Cover and cook over medium heat for 30 minutes. Add the potatoes; cook for 15 minutes. Add the bananas, peanuts, cream and molasses; cook 15 minutes longer. Taste for seasoning.

Makes 6 to 8 servings

From: *The Art of South American Cookery*

Poultry

Senegalese Couscous

Ingredients

1½ fryer chickens, cut up
4 medium onions, chopped
½ cup peanut oil
3 bay leaves
1¼ teaspoons turmeric, divided
2 chicken bouillon cubes, dissolved in 2 cups boiling
    water
2 carrots, cut up
1 turnip, cut up
1 small cabbage, cut up
1 to 2 teaspoons cayenne
Salt
3 or 4 zucchini, cut up
1 eggplant, peeled and cut up
1 (1-pound) can chick peas, drained
1 pound instant couscous
¼ cup butter, melted
5 tablespoons raisins

Brown chicken and onions in hot oil until golden. Add bay leaves, 1 teaspoon turmeric, bouillon and enough water to barely cover. Simmer 20 minutes. Add carrots and turnip and continue simmering 15 minutes. Add cabbage, cayenne, salt, zucchini, and eggplant and simmer 20 minutes longer or until all ingredients are tender. (Add bouillon or water as needed.) Add chick peas. If sauce is too watery, reduce over high heat, stirring frequently.

Meanwhile, cook *couscous*. First, wash grains very quickly with only enough water to barely wet. Strain very carefully in a clean, soft kitchen towel.

Melt butter and add ¼ teaspoon turmeric. Mix with *couscous* in a bowl along with the raisins which have been softened in hot water and drained.

Line a *couscous* steamer (or colander that will fit into a large dutch oven) with a dry cloth. Add *couscous* mixture and place colander over boiling water in the dutch oven so the *couscous* is steamed without getting wet. Cover and steam about 15 minutes.

Serve *couscous* on a large dish with chicken around it, and garnished with a few vegetables. Pass the sauce separately in one bowl and the rest of the vegetables in another.

Makes 6 servings

**From: Best of Regional African Cooking
        (Senegal)**

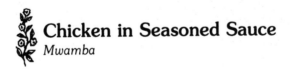

Chicken in Seasoned Sauce
Mwamba

Ingredients

1 chicken, cut up, or 2 pounds beef or lamb, or
        1½ pounds fish fillets (fresh or thawed frozen)
Salt
Oil
2 large onions, cut up
2 to 4 chili peppers, mashed, or ½ to 1 tablespoon dried
        crushed red pepper
6 or 7 tomatoes, peeled, seeded, and mashed

Season chicken, meat, or fish well with salt. In hot oil in a heavy stewing pan, sauté chicken, meat, or fish with the onions until well-browned. Add chili peppers, tomatoes, and enough water to barely cover. Simmer until tender and nicely cooked.

Chicken *Mwamba* is usually served with boiled rice. Fish, lamb, or beef *Mwamba* is frequently accompanied by fried plantain.

Variation:

Some recipes include peanuts in this dish. Mix ¼ to ⅓ cup peanut butter with a little boiling water until smooth and add to stew 15 to 20 minutes before it is done.

Makes 4 to 6 servings

From: **Best of Regional African Cooking**
       (Congo)

Gabon Chicken Stew

Ingredients

1½ cups palm or hazelnuts
1½ cups water
¼ to ½ cup palm or peanut oil
2 to 3 chili peppers or ½ to 1 tablespoon crushed
     red pepper
1 teaspoon salt
1 clove garlic, minced
2 medium onions, thinly sliced
1 frying chicken, cut up

Process nuts in blender until very finely ground. In a heavy stewing pan, combine all ingredients (except chicken), and mix well. Add chicken, turning pieces in the liquid so they are nicely coated. Cover and simmer over a low heat until the chicken is tender, 45 minutes to 1 hour, stirring occasionally. If necessary, add water to prevent scorching.

Makes 4 to 6 servings

From: ***Best of Regional African Cooking***
(Gabon)

 # Ugandan Chicken Stew

Ingredients

1 fryer chicken, cut up
4 tablespoons oil
1 large onion, sliced
2 or 3 tomatoes, peeled and cut in eighths
2 potatoes, peeled and sliced
1 teaspoon salt
½ teaspoon pepper

In a heavy stewing pan, sauté chicken pieces in hot oil until nicely browned. Add onion, tomatoes, potatoes, salt, pepper, and enough water to just cover. Cover pan and simmer until chicken is cooked, 45 minutes to 1 hour.

Makes 4 servings

From: ***Best of Regional African Cooking***
(Uganda)

Tanzanian Chicken Stew

Ingredients

1 fryer chicken, cut up
2 onions
Salt
3 tablespoons oil
3 tomatoes, peeled and sliced
2 cloves garlic, minced
1 or 2 chili peppers
3 whole cloves
2 teaspoons curry powder
2 green peppers, seeded and cut into strips
1 cup coconut milk
2 potatoes, peeled and sliced

Place chicken in a stewing pan with one of the onions (whole). Season with salt and add enough water to barely cover. Cook, uncovered, about 15 minutes at a moderately high heat so stock reduces to about 1 cup.

Meanwhile, slice remaining onion. Sauté in hot oil until yellow. Add tomatoes, garlic, chili pepper, cloves, curry powder, green peppers, and salt to taste. Sauté about 5 minutes. Drain chicken, reserving stock. Add chicken to onion mixture and fry about 5 minutes, turning chicken to brown evenly. Add 1 cup chicken stock and ½ cup coconut milk and the potatoes. Simmer, uncovered, 30 minutes, stirring occasionally. Add remaining coconut milk and continue simmering until all is tender, 10 to 12 minutes more. Remove chicken pieces to serving platter. Stir stew to break up and slightly mash the potatoes. Serve over the chicken.

Makes 4 servings

From: ***Best of Regional African Cooking***
(Tanzania)

Chicken with Pineapple in the Old Style

Ingredients

6 joints or quarters of frying chicken
Lemon or lime juice
Salt and pepper
All-purpose flour
2 tablespoons butter
1 onion, minced
3 tablespoons currants
1 teaspoon finely grated lemon peel
1 teaspoon brown sugar
2 tomatoes, skinned and pulped
Pineapple sauce

for the Pineapple sauce

1 ripe pineapple, peeled and cored*
1 tablespoon rum
Chop and crush pineapple and mix to a pulp with all its juice in an electric blender. Simmer until reduced to ¼ then stir in rum.

Brush chicken with lemon juice, sprinkle with salt and pepper and dust in flour. Heat butter and brown chicken in it. Reduce heat and cover pan closely. Cook gently until chicken is tender. Then add onion, currants, lemon peel, brown sugar, tomatoes. Season to taste. Blend thoroughly and cook gently for a further 10 minutes. Pour sauce over chicken and serve.

*TIPS:
1 (12-ounce) can pineapple may be substituted.

Makes 6 servings

From: *Cooking the Caribbean Way*
(Cuba)

Apricot Chicken

Ingredients

1½ pounds chicken pieces
1 packet French onion soup
1 cup apricot nectar (juice)
10 dried apricots

Place chicken into a shallow casserole. Sprinkle soup powder over the pieces, then pour on apricot juice. Cook in a 325 degree oven for 50 minutes. Add chopped dried apricots and cook an additional 10 minutes.

Makes 4 to 6 servings

From: *Good Food from Australia*

 # Chicken on Skewers
Sateh

Ingredients

Chicken (or lamb or pork)
Salt and pepper
Sateh sauce (see recipe below)

for the Sateh sauce
4 tablespoons peanut butter
½ teaspoon crushed red chili pepper
2 teaspoons molasses
1 tablespoon soy sauce
1 clove garlic, minced
Few drops lemon juice

162

Mix the peanut butter with 8 tablespoons hot water, stir in all the other ingredients, and simmer for 5 minutes. Cover the Satehs with the hot sauce (sufficient for 8 pieces) just before serving.

Cut the chicken (or lamb or pork) in bite-size cubes, rub with salt and pepper, and let stand for 15 minutes. Thread 5 or 6 pieces onto a skewer. Baste with oil and roast in a slow oven (325 degrees), turning frequently, or grill on a barbecue.

Serving sizes vary

From: **The Art of Dutch Cooking**
(Indonesia)

Roast Duck
Sieu Ngaap

Ingredients

1 clove garlic, crushed
4 teaspoons *saang see jeung* (sauce)
½ teaspoon *heung new fun* spice
½ teaspoon pepper
1 teaspoon sugar
1 teaspoon salt
1 tablespoon soya sauce
2 tablespoons sherry
1 tender fat duck complete with neck and head
(6 to 8 pounds)
1 teaspoon honey

Make a sauce by mixing crushed garlic, *saang see jeung* (aromatic sauce), *heung new fun*, pepper, sugar, salt, soya sauce, and sherry. Pour sauce into duck and rub thoroughly all over inner surface. Sew up opening and wipe entire outer surface of duck clean. Gripping duck by neck over the hole in its neck, blow air into space between skin and bony neck portion until duck becomes puffed to the limit. Grip neck below hole immediately so that air will not escape, and then tie string around neck securely.

Dissolve honey in 1 cup boiling water. Hold duck by neck over basin and pour honeyed water over duck about eight times. Meanwhile, heat oven moderately hot and place duck in it upon shallow roasting pan breast side up about 3 to 4 inches from heat. When entire top surface of duck turns to a smooth rich reddish brown—after 15 to 20 minutes—turn duck over, and roast about 20 minutes. Brush surface with drippings periodically during roasting. Turn off heat and allow to roast in heat of oven about 10 to 15 minutes. Place duck on rack to drain and cool. Pour all drippings into bowl to use as sauce for Roast Duck.

When duck is cool, cut open threads and pour sauce into bowl containing drippings. Split duck along spine into 2 portions. Remove legs at thigh joints, and remove wings at shoulder joints. Carefully tear off breast meat. Use breast meat and thigh meat for Pineapple Duck. Use neck, head, bones, lower wings, and legs for Roast Duck Congee. Use drumstick, wings, and back area of duck for Roast Duck. Chop these portions into neat slices about ½ to ¾-inch wide, arrange slices on a platter, pour sauce from roast duck over and serve.

Makes 4 servings

From: *The Joy of Chinese Cooking*

164

Breast of Chicken Brabançonne
Médaillons de Volaille Brabançonne

Ingredients

4 to 6 chicken breasts
1 carrot, chopped
1 stalk celery, chopped
½ bay leaf
Pepper and salt
8 endive stalks
Juice of 1 lemon
½ stick butter
1 jigger cognac more or less

Poach chicken in 2 cups water with carrot, celery, bay leaf, pepper and salt. Remove chicken and reserve broth for other uses. Bring endive to a boil in 2 quarts water; reduce heat, add lemon juice. Simmer for 20 minutes. Pour off liquid from endive but do not drain completely. Place in skillet or flameproof casserole with butter and chicken and braise over medium to high heat until edges of vegetables and meat are lightly browned. Taste and correct seasoning.

Warm cognac slightly. Bring casserole to the table. Ignite cognac and pour into casserole.

Makes 4 servings

From: *A Belgian Cookbook*

165

 # Welsh Chicken

This is a dish for a boiling fowl, and this recipe comes from *Croeso Cymreig*:

Ingredients

Chicken (1 or 2)
½ pound bacon (15 slices)
2 large leeks
½ pound carrots
2 tablespoons butter
About ¼ cup all-purpose flour
1 small cabbage
Bunch of mixed herbs
Salt and pepper
1 cup stock
Dripping

Young birds need not be used for this dish. Truss them as for boiling. Cut the bacon, leeks, and carrots into dice. Put them into a casserole with the butter and fry for a few minutes, stir in the flour until it thickens and browns. Place the chicken in the thickened sauce.* Wash and cut up a small cabbage and put it in the casserole with the chicken, add a bunch of herbs, and sprinkle in salt and pepper. Add the stock, put some small lumps of dripping or butter on the bird, cover, and simmer for 2 to 3 hours. When serving, make a bed of the cooked cabbage on a dish and place the bird on it. Garnish with the carrots and pour the liquor over the cabbage.

*TIPS:

Thicken the sauce at the end of the cooking time. Also, do not add the cabbage until the chicken is nearly cooked, otherwise it is flabby and unattractive.

Makes 4 to 6 servings

From: Traditional Food from Wales

Chicken Polish Style

Ingredients

1 young chicken,
   quartered
Salt
4 cups water
2 stalks celery, cut
3 dried mushrooms, chopped
2 carrots, sliced
Parsley, chopped
1 tablespoon butter
1 tablespoon all-purpose flour
2 egg yolks
½ cup white wine

Cook the quartered chicken in salted water. Remove chicken and reserve stock. Bring stock to a boil, adding celery, mushrooms, carrots and parsley. Stew until tender for about 1 hour or less. Melt 1 tablespoon of butter and blend in 1 tablespoon of flour, adding to it the remaining chicken stock and cook until it thickens. Then, gradually pour in egg yolks and wine and add chicken. Simmer for a few minutes but do not boil. Serve with boiled or mashed potatoes.

Makes 4 servings

From: *Old Warsaw Cookbook*

Roast Fowl
(The Old Cape Way, in a Baking-Pot)

Ingredients

2 fresh young fowls
2 tablespoons mixed butter and fat
A glass of wine
A few slices bacon
Salt and pepper

After having carefully picked, and singed the small feathers by burning a clean paper over the fowl, cut off the neck and skewer the skin down over the back. Cut off the claws, dip the legs in boiling water, scrape them, and turn the pinions under; run a skewer through them and the middle of the leg through the body, to the pinion and leg on the other side. The liver and gizzard should be placed in the wings, the liver on one side, the gizzard on the other. Tie the legs by passing a trussing-needle, threaded with twine, through the backbone, and securing on the other side. Now place your chickens, with the breast down, in a baking-pot; if not quite young and tender put half of water in a baking-pot, also a little of the butter and fat.

After 1 hour, turn the chickens over, put over them some more butter and fat, and a glass of wine. Put on the outside of the lid of the baking-pot some coals of wood fire. When the chickens are nice and brown, send them in. Garnish with some fried bacon, and salt and pepper to taste. Serve with bread sauce. Time, about 1½ hours.

Makes 8 servings

From: *Traditional South African Cookery*

Pojarskiya Kotleti with Chicken

Ingredients

3½- to 4-pound roasting chicken
2 cups crumbled bread from a French loaf 1 day old
½ cup sweet cream
½ teaspoon salt
1 tablespoon vodka or gin
7 tablespoons butter, divided
1 egg yolk
1 small tablespoon all-purpose flour

Remove the skin from the uncooked chicken. Remove all the meat from bones and discard all gristle. Put the chicken meat twice through a meat grinder. Crumble the soft inside part from a long French loaf. Soak 2 cups of the crumbs in the cream, then squeeze dry. Combine the bread with the ground chicken, salt, vodka or gin, and 2 tablespoons of the butter, creamed. Mix thoroughly, then add the egg yolk. It is best to do the mixing with your hands.

Turn the mixture out onto a wet wooden board. Divide into 12 parts. Form each part into a small, thick oval cake. Sprinkle these with flour and fry them immediately in very hot butter until golden-brown.

A perfect Pojarski kotlet ought to be so buttery you'll have to watch out it doesn't spray you when you stick your fork in it.

At Pojarski's tavern the original recipe for these kotleti says they should be made with the meat of hazel hens or young partridges, supplemented by a small amount of finely chopped fillet of beef.

Makes 4 servings

From: *The Best of Russian Cooking*

Roast Turkey
Traditional American

Ingredients

1 turkey, dressed and cleaned
Salt

for the Stuffing
Breadcrumbs as desired
Milk or water
Chicken stock or pea soup
1 egg, optional
1 pound sausage meat, minced
1 large onion, chopped
Stalks of celery, chopped
Several apples, chopped
Sage
Parsley, chopped
Sprinkling of poultry seasoning

In making stuffing, the creative cook often first cleans out the refrigerator! Using either dry breadcrumbs or small torn pieces of moist bread as a base, almost anything can be used as additional flavoring for stuffing and for the turkey itself. Although milk or water are the standard wetting agents, chicken stock or pea soup lend delightful flavors to the mixture. An egg is a cohesive or binding influence in a stuffing and may be used or not, depending upon the texture desired.

In the above, the sausage meat is browned in a frying pan until it is crumbly and partially cooked. Onions, celery, apples are added and browned. Remove from the fire and combine with bread and sage, parsley and poultry seasonings. An unbeaten egg may be mixed into the stuffing at this point and enough liquid to make a wet but not sloppy concoction. If desired, the giblets may be cooked in water and when tender, chopped and added. The water in which they are cooked makes a good liquid agent for the stuffing.

To prepare a cleaned bird for stuffing, pat salt onto the inside of the cavities. Now fill with the stuffing. When the bird is well-packed, secure the openings with needle and thread or skewers and twine laced over them.

The bird will bake well and will be easier to handle if the wings and legs are bound close to the body with stout thread or string. It is then placed in a shallow roasting pan.

There are 2 ways to roast a turkey in time for a noontime or early afternoon Thanksgiving dinner. By the first, the cook rises at dawn to prepare the turkey. The turkey should be coated with a mixture of butter and flour and then roasted in a moderate oven (350 degrees). The cook should calculate to allow 25 minutes per pound if the turkey weighs under 12 pounds, or 20 minutes per pound if it weighs more than that. Baste the turkey with butter and water every 15 minutes or as often as can be remembered during the morning hours.

By the second method the cook stuffs and prepares the turkey the night before Thanksgiving. Just before going to bed coat the turkey with salad oil and cover it with metal foil. Then place in a 250 degree oven, and go to bed until your normal rising hour the next morning. Remove turkey from oven and let it rest until almost dinner time.

Remove the foil and brown the turkey in a 450 degree oven to serve hot from the oven.

Makes numerous servings and leftovers
depending on turkey size

From: *Old Warsaw Cookbook*
(American)

Pilav Pie
Yufkah Pilav

Ingredients

2 cups long grain rice
1 small chicken, 2½ pounds
5 cups water
2 carrots, scraped, 1 quartered, 1 grated
     coarsely (divided)
2 onions, skinned, 1 quartered, 1 grated
     coarsely (divided)
2 sprigs parsley, chopped
Salt
6 peppercorns
12 tablespoons butter, divided
2 ounces slivered almonds
Pepper
8 sheets Phyllo pastry*

Place rice in a bowl, add 1 tablespoon salt, and cover with hot water. Stir and allow to cool. Drain and set aside.

Preheat oven to 350 degrees. Clean and wash chicken, place in a stock pot with 5 cups of water and cut up carrot, onion, parsley, salt, and peppercorns. Bring to a boil, cover, and cook over medium heat until chicken is tender, about 45 minutes. Remove chicken from pot. Cool, take off skin and remove bones. Separate meat into 2- or 3-inch long pieces. Set aside. Strain stock and save.

In a heavy saucepan sauté grated onion with 9 tablespoons of butter over medium heat for 5 minutes, stirring constantly. Add grated carrot and sauté for 5 minutes more. Add almonds and continue to sauté another 3 minutes. Add chicken pieces and cook 5 minutes, stirring occasionally. Add pepper.

Bring 3 cups of the chicken stock to a boil in a saucepan. Add the chicken mixture and bring to a boil again. Add the rice, stirring carefully not to break it. Cover and cook without stirring over high heat for 5 minutes. Turn heat to medium and cook until small holes appear on the surface of rice, but not all the broth is absorbed, about 10 minutes.

While rice is cooking, grease a 4-quart casserole with half the remaining butter. Line it with pastry sheets, covering the bottom with one end and leaving the other end hanging out over the rim of the casserole. The sheets should overlap so that the entire casserole, bottom and sides, is covered with pastry sheets.

Place half-cooked rice mixture in the casserole. Fold pastry sheets over rice, like a package. Butter top with remaining butter. Bake until top is golden-brown, about 25 to 30 minutes.

Remove from oven. Invert on a round serving platter. Cut through the crust with a sharp knife, and serve together with the rice.

*TIPS:
Serve warm as an appetizer for formal dinners or as a luncheon course with a Romaine lettuce salad.

Makes 8 to 10 servings

From: *The Art of Turkish Cooking*

Chicken Breasts, Asturian-Style
Pollo Ovetense

The word *ovetense* means from Oviedo, which is the principal city of Asturias. This is a simple chicken dish from this cider region of northern Spain. Like many other such dishes, it can be made in advance and reheated, adding the cream, grapes and croutons before serving.

Ingredients

4 chicken breast portions, skinned
All-purpose flour (for dredging)
2 tablespoons sunflower oil, or other light oil
2 tablespoons butter
1 medium onion, chopped
1 clove garlic, chopped (optional)
1 tablespoon chopped parsley
3 teaspoons paprika
Salt and pepper
1 cup cider
2 tablespoons light cream
12 grapes, deseeded and halved
2 tablespoons *migas* or croutons

Dredge the chicken breasts generously with seasoned flour.

Heat the oil and butter in a large, shallow pan and sauté the chicken until lightly brown all over. Remove the chicken and keep warm.

Add the onion and garlic to the pan and cook until soft. Stir in the parsley, paprika and salt and pepper to taste. Then pour in the cider, bring to a boil, stirring gently and add a little water if necessary. Lower heat and return the chicken to the casserole. Cover and allow to simmer gently for about 10 to 15

174

minutes. Turn heat to very low (do not allow to boil) and stir in the cream, grapes and croutons. Serve immediately.

Makes 4 servings

From: *A Spanish Family Cookbook*

Chicken with Oranges
Gallina con Naranjas

Ingredients

1 (6-pound) roasting chicken, disjointed
2 cups orange juice
1½ cups minced onions
¼ teaspoon dried ground chili peppers
1 bay leaf
4 tablespoons butter
2 teaspoons salt
2 tablespoons all-purpose flour
½ teaspoon sugar
2 oranges, thinly sliced

Wash and dry the chicken. In a bowl (not metal) mix the orange juice, onions, chili peppers, and bay leaf. Marinate the chicken in the mixture overnight in the refrigerator. Baste frequently.

When ready to cook, drain the chicken, reserving the marinade. Melt the butter in a casserole; brown the chicken in it. Sprinkle with the salt, flour, and sugar, stirring until flour browns. Add the marinade. Cover and cook over low heat for 1½ hours, or until tender. Taste for seasoning. Garnish with the orange slices.

Makes 4 to 6 servings

**From: *The Art of South American Cookery*
(Ecuador)**

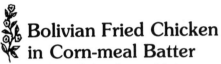

Bolivian Fried Chicken in Corn-meal Batter
Pollitos Salteados en Maíz

Ingredients

2 egg yolks
1 cup corn meal
1 cup grated Cheddar cheese
1½ teaspoons salt
½ teaspoon white pepper
2 egg whites, stiffly beaten
2 (2½-pound) fryers, disjointed
¾ cup salad oil

Beat the egg yolks; stir in the corn meal, cheese, salt, and pepper. Fold in the egg whites. Dip the chicken pieces in the mixture, coating them well.

Heat the oil in skillet and fry the chicken in it until browned and tender.

Makes 6 to 8 servings

From: *The Art of South American Cookery*
(Bolivia)

177

Chicken in Red Wine
Pollo al Cazador

Ingredients

½ cup all-purpose flour
2½ teaspoons salt
¾ teaspoon freshly ground black pepper
2 (3-pound) fryers, disjointed
⅓ cup olive oil
8 small white onions
1 cup peeled, chopped tomatoes
½ pound mushrooms, sliced
1 cup sliced green peppers
1 bay leaf
½ teaspoon orégano
1½ cups dry red wine
1½ cups drained canned chick-peas

Mix together the flour, salt, and pepper; toss the chicken in the mixture. Heat the oil in a casserole or Dutch oven; brown the chicken in it. Add the onions, tomatoes, and mushrooms; cook over medium heat for 10 minutes. Add the green peppers, bay leaf, orégano, wine, and chick-peas. Cover and cook over low heat for 1 hour, or until chicken is tender. Taste for seasoning.

Makes 6 to 8 servings

From: The Art of South American Cookery
(Uruguay)

178

Pigeons in Red Wine
Palomas con Vino Rojo

Ingredients

4 pigeons or squabs
2 teaspoons salt
½ teaspoon freshly ground black pepper
3 tablespoons olive oil
¼ cup orange juice
1 tablespoon lemon juice
2 tablespoons butter
¾ cup dry red wine
1 bay leaf
¼ teaspoon marjoram
1 cup sliced, stuffed green olives

Wash and dry the birds; rub inside and out with the salt, pepper, olive oil, orange and lemon juice. Refrigerate overnight.

Melt the butter in a casserole. Brown the drained birds (reserve any liquid) in it. Add the liquid, wine, bay leaf, and marjoram. Cover and cook over low heat for 20 minutes, or until almost tender. Add the olives and cook 10 minutes longer. Taste for seasoning.

Makes 4 servings

From: *The Art of South American Cookery*
(Chile)

Fish & Seafood

 **Fish Calalou**

Ingredients

2 large tomatoes
1 pound eggplant
1 large onion, finely chopped
2 tablespoons peanut oil
1 pound fresh fish fillets, cut in pieces
1 (10-ounce) package frozen okra, thawed
½ to 1 teaspoon cayenne
½ green pepper, sliced
¼ cup very finely chopped peanuts or chunk-style
     peanut butter
Salt

Peel tomatoes and eggplant, but leave whole.

In a stewing pan, brown half the chopped onion in oil. Add fish fillets and brown. Reduce heat and simmer 15 minutes. Remove fish and set aside. Add whole vegetables, cayenne, green pepper, and chopped peanuts or peanut butter. Add enough water to cover. Simmer, covered, on a low fire about 30 minutes. Remove whole vegetables and mash together into a purée. Return vegetable purée to stewing pot, along with the remaining chopped onions and fish. Season with salt and simmer a few minutes to heat and blend flavors.

Makes 6 servings

From: *Best of Regional African Cooking*
     (Ivory Coast)

Pickled Fish

Ingredients

2 pounds white fish
2 cups water
½ cup vinegar
1 tablespoon lemon or lime juice
6 to 8 cloves
Pinch ground ginger
½ teaspoon ground mace
½ teaspoon dry mustard
3 bay leaves, crushed
2 onions, chopped
Pinch salt
⅛ teaspoon black pepper
Dash Angostura bitters
1 head lettuce
Green sauce (see recipe below)

for the **Green sauce**
4 tablespoons sour cream
8 tablespoons mayonnaise
1 tablespoon watercress or spinach, finely chopped
½ clove garlic, crushed
Lemon or lime juice
Generous dash Tabasco
Mix together the sour cream, mayonnaise, watercress (or spinach), garlic, lemon or lime juice, and the Tabasco. Whip and rub through a sieve or mix in a blender. Serve chilled with cold fish, especially lobster.

Variations
Add 1 teaspoon chervil, tarragon or basil.

183

Simmer fish in water until cooked. Remove bone and flake it, then pour vinegar and lemon juice over, adding enough of the liquid in which fish was cooked to cover. Add cloves, ground ginger, mace, mustard, bay leaves, onion, salt and pepper and bring slowly to a boil. Add the Angostura and simmer for 20 minutes. Allow to cool, then drain fish and stand in the refrigerator for 3 hours.

Wash and drain lettuce, place in the bottom of salad bowl. Fill the bowl with fish and serve with green sauce.

Makes 4 to 6 servings

From: ***Cooking the Caribbean Way***
       (Barbados)

 **Dried Fish**
Hogada

Ingredients

1 pound dried fish of any kind
4 tablespoons mustard oil
½ teaspoon asafoetida water or 4 cloves garlic, crushed
1½ tablespoons red chili powder
1 teaspoon turmeric powder
3 cups water
1 teaspoon ginger powder
1 teaspoon fennel powder
½ teaspoon vari masala (spice cake)
1 teaspoon salt

Scrape the fish clean, removing the blackened film of skin, if any. Wash and pat dry. If the fish is too large, cut into medium-sized pieces. Heat oil in a pan. Before it starts smoking, put in the fish. Stir-fry until it has been sizzling for about 5 minutes. Add the asafoetida water or crushed garlic, chili and turmeric powder, and 3 cups water. When boiling, put in the ginger and fennel powder. Add vari masala and salt. Simmer until the fish is done. It should not be too soft. Kashmiris like their *hogada* to be chewable and slightly crunchy.

Makes 8 servings

From: *The Best of Kashmiri Cooking*

 Issykul Fried Trout

Ingredients

4 fresh trout
All-purpose flour (for dredging)
About 6 tablespoons vegetable oil
Salt and freshly ground black pepper
1 small onion, finely chopped
½ cup shredded white radish (daikon)
1 small pale green Italian frying pepper, cored, seeded
       and cut in thin strips
2 tomatoes, peeled, seeded and chopped
2 tablespoons tomato paste
2 tablespoons chopped parsley

Clean the trout and rinse well with cold water inside and out. Dry with paper towels and dredge with flour on all sides, shaking off the excess. In a skillet large enough to hold the 4 fish comfortably, heat 3 tablespoons of the vegetable oil until very hot but not smoking, and fry the trout in it on medium heat for a few minutes on each side until crisp and golden-brown. Add more oil if necessary. Remove the trout and put them on a plate, sprinkle them lightly with salt and pepper, and set aside.

In a separate pan, heat another 3 tablespoons vegetable oil and sauté the onions over medium heat until golden, stirring them well. Add the shredded daikon and green pepper and cook for another 2 to 3 minutes. Stir in the tomatoes and tomato paste, and mix well. Add salt and black pepper to taste, and cook for another 5 minutes. Add 1 to 2 tablespoons of water until the mixture becomes very thick.

Return the fish to the pan, cover, and simmer on low heat for 5 minutes. Each trout should be served covered with the vegetable sauce and sprinkled with the chopped parsley.

The fish can be served with green peas and quartered tomatoes.

Makes 4 servings

From: *Kirghiz Recipes*

 Crab Creole

Ingredients

4 small crabs
¼ pound bread crumbs
2 red peppers, chopped finely
Chervil, chopped
Pinch mace
Cayenne pepper
Salt
Dash sherry
Lime or lemon juice
Clove garlic, crushed

186

Remove flesh from shells and put crab meat in a basin. Mash with a fork, adding enough breadcrumbs to make a paste. Add the peppers, herbs, salt, sherry, juice, and garlic, beating in all ingredients.

Scrub the empty shells, and fill with the mixture. Sprinkle with remaining breadcrumbs, dot with butter and bake in a moderate oven (350 degrees) until well-browned.

Makes 4 servings

From: ***Cooking the Caribbean Way***
(Guadeloupe)

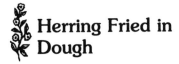 ## Herring Fried in Dough

Ingredients

6 herrings, boned and cleaned
2 eggs, separated
1 tablespoon sour cream
1½ tablespoons all-purpose
    flour
5 tablespoons butter (for frying)

Cut herrings in half, lengthwise. Beat the egg yolks, add sour cream, flour and beaten egg whites, mixing gently. Dip herring halves in the dough and fry on both sides in butter.

Makes 6 servings

From: ***Lithuanian Cookbook***

Lobster Curry, Gorda Style

Ingredients

3 small lobsters
2 tablespoons olive oil
1¾ sticks butter
1 mild onion, finely chopped
1 green pepper, finely chopped
1 apple, finely chopped
1 tablespoon grated coconut
3 tablespoons white wine
3 tablespoons curry powder
1 teaspoon turmeric powder
2 tablespoons tomato paste
Stock
Salt
1 cup thick white sauce (see recipe below)
1 tablespoon chutney

for the White sauce
2 tablespoons butter or margarine
2 tablespoons all-purpose flour
1 cup milk
Seasoning
Melt butter or margarine in saucepan, stir in the flour until there is a smooth paste. Add the milk, little by little, stirring all the time to prevent burning. Season to taste.

Cut the tails from the lobsters and divide each lobster into 6. Fry it in oil and butter until light brown. Add onion, pepper, apple, coconut and wine and cook for a further 5 minutes.

Transfer to a casserole and stir in curry powder, turmeric, tomato paste and stock to cover. Season to taste and bake in a very moderate oven (350 degrees) for 30 minutes. Take out the lobster pieces and extract meat from the tails. Set aside. Reduce sauce by half, thicken with white sauce and stir in chutney. Season to taste, add lobster meat, coat thoroughly then heat through in the oven. Serve with hot boiled rice.

Makes 6 servings

From: ***Cooking the Caribbean Way***
(British Virgin Islands)

Fish Fillets in Coconut Milk Sauce
Muqueca Bahiana

Ingredients

3 onions, divided
2 cloves garlic, minced (optional)
1½ teaspoons salt
Juice of 2 lemons
6 fish fillets (halibut, lake trout)
4 tomatoes, peeled and chopped
2 green peppers, chopped
½ cup olive oil
1½ cups coconut milk, divided
2 tablespoons *dendê*, corn, or peanut oil
1 cup hot water
Salt
2 tablespoons all-purpose flour

Chop 2 of the onions, mix with garlic, salt, and lemon juice, and marinate the fish in this for 2 hours. Put over flame in heavy pan. Add the tomatoes, the green peppers, the other onion, chopped, the olive oil, ¾ cup of the coconut milk, the *dendê* or other oil, and cook for 25 minutes, or until fish is tender. Lift the fish out carefully onto a hot platter and keep hot. Add the hot water and a little salt to the mixture in the pan, and put all through a sieve. Bring to a boil and add the rest of the coconut milk and thicken the sauce with the flour mixed with a little cold water. Pour sauce over fish fillets and serve at once.

Makes 6 servings

From: *The Art of Brazilian Cookery*

Salmon Pie
Lohipiirakka

Ingredients

***for the* Pastry**
12 tablespoons butter or margarine (1½ sticks)
2 cups all-purpose flour
½ pound cream cheese or Neufchâtel cheese
Blend the butter and flour together until the mixture resembles coarse meal. Work in the cream cheese until the dough holds together in a ball. Wrap and chill for 30 minutes.

190

for the **Filling**
1 tablespoon butter or oil
1 small onion, peeled and chopped
¾ cup uncooked rice
1½ cups chicken broth or water
2 cups canned or fresh salmon
2 hard-boiled eggs, peeled and coarsely chopped
½ cup chopped fresh dill, divided
Salt and pepper
2 tablespoons milk or cream
1 tablespoon lemon juice

for the **Glaze**
1 egg yolk
2 tablespoons milk

Melt the butter in a saucepan and add the chopped onion. Cook until onion is soft. Add the rice and stir until rice is coated with butter. Add the chicken broth or water, bring to boil, cover, and let cook over low heat for 18 minutes.

While the rice is cooking, remove the skin and bones from the salmon, coarsely flake it, and add the chopped eggs and half of the chopped dill. Sprinkle with salt to taste.

After the rice is cooked, fluff it with a fork and stir in the rest of the chopped dill. If the mixture seems dry, add a couple of tablespoons of milk or cream, and sprinkle with pepper and salt, if needed.

Preheat oven to 350 degrees. Divide the pastry dough in roughly 2 equal pieces, making 1 part slightly bigger than the other. Roll the smaller piece on top of a parchment paper the size of a cookie sheet (dampen the surface underneath with water to prevent slipping) to a size approximately 6 × 10 inches. Transfer the paper with the dough on it onto a cookie sheet. Spoon the rice mixture evenly over the dough, leaving about 1 inch of dough visible all around. Spoon the salmon mixture evenly over the rice and sprinkle lemon juice over the salmon. Roll the other half of dough into a slightly larger sheet than the first one and transfer it with the aid of a rolling pin on top of the salmon. Press the edges firmly together with the aid of a fork. You may decorate the surface by lightly drawing the tines of the fork over the surface, crisscrossing both ways. Beat the egg yolk with the milk and brush the loaf before baking. Bake for about 45 minutes, or until golden-brown. Serve hot in slices, with melted butter or sour cream.

Makes 4 to 6 servings

From: *The Best of Finnish Cooking*

Five Willows Fish
Ngung Lao Yü

Ingredients

1 firm cucumber
1 carrot
1 piece young ginger
1 sweet pickle
½ Spanish onion
Salt
2 tablespoons sugar
½ cup vinegar
Water
1 (2 to 3 pound) red snapper
1 tablespoon *hoy sien jeung*
2 teaspoons cornstarch
2 crushed cloves garlic
¼ teaspoon white pepper
2 tablespoons salad oil

Slice cucumber in two lengthwise, remove soft pulp, and then slice into 2-inch long matchsticks. Scrape carrot and slice into 2-inch long matchsticks. Slice young ginger and sweet pickle into needlelike sticks. Mince onion fine. Sprinkle 1 teaspoon salt over vegetables, let seep in for 10 minutes, and then add 4 to 6 teaspoons sugar, ½ cup vinegar, and ½ cup water. Allow ingredients to marinate about ½ hour.

Meanwhile, heat 2 quarts water in large, flattish, lidded pot. When boiling, add 2 tablespoons salt and 2 tablespoons oil. Raise heat so water comes to rapid boil, place fish carefully in water, cover pot with lid, and then turn off fire entirely, thus allowing fish to cook in heat of water (about ½ hour).

Drain vegetables and place in dry dish. Make a sauce, using vinegar mixture in which vegetables marinated (add sugar to taste if necessary), 1 tablespoon *hoy sien jeung*, 2 teaspoons cornstarch dissolved in a little water. Heat a little oil in a pan, fry 2 crushed cloves of garlic, and then add sauce and simmer until it thickens.

If the fish is too cool after soaking, reheat rapidly in same water, take out, sprinkle lightly with salt and white pepper, then cover with layer of marinated vegetables, pour sauce over this, and then finally pour 2 tablespoons salad oil over sauce.

Makes 4 servings

From: *The Joy of Chinese Cooking*

Scalloped Lobster
Kreef

Ingredients

1 cup milk
1 tablespoon fine flour
4 tablespoons butter
3 pounds lobster
1 teaspoon salt
½ teaspoon or less cayenne
1 tablespoon chopped parsley
½ cup stale breadcrumbs

Let the milk boil, rub the flour and butter together and stir into the boiling milk, let it boil up nice and smooth for a sauce. Boil the lobster, open and cut the meat into dice-shaped pieces. Put a layer of white sauce at the bottom of the baking-dish—then a layer of lobster seasoned with salt and cayenne, and a sprinkling of parsley and breadcrumbs, adding sauce and lobster alternately until the dish is filled; the *last* layer should be white sauce, sprinkled with breadcrumbs and a little melted butter on the top.

Put in a quick oven to brown and get thoroughly warm. It can be replaced in the shell to be served—or left in the pie-dish, the outside of which should be garnished with frilled papers.

Makes 4 servings

From: *Traditional South African Cookery*

Kedgeree

Ingredients

¼ pound cooked rice
½ pound cooked finnan haddock or white fish
1 hard-boiled egg
4 tablespoons butter
Cayenne pepper
Nutmeg
Salt

Wash, boil, and dry the rice. Remove all skin and bones from the fish, and chop roughly. Separate the white from the yolk of the egg; chop the white roughly; rub the yolk through a wire sieve.

Melt the butter in a stewpan; add the rice, fish, and white of egg. When thoroughly heated, season with cayenne pepper, nutmeg, and salt. Pile on a hot dish, and decorate with the sieved yolk.

Makes 2 servings

From: *Traditional Food from Scotland*

 # Herring Filet Tidbit

Ingredients

4 eggs, divided
½ can "Sill I Dill"
½ cup soft white bread crumbs

Hard boil 3 eggs and then chop fine. Mash "Sill I Dill" to a fine paste, and mix with bread crumbs, then with eggs. Add 1 egg-yolk (raw) and, last, stiffly beaten egg white. Drop teaspoon of mixture in oil to brown.

Makes 4 servings

From: **The Best of Smorgasbord Cooking**

 **Coquilles St. Jacques**
Scallops

Ingredients

1 onion, chopped
Olive oil
½ pound mushrooms, sliced
1 pound scallops
2 sections garlic
Bread crumbs
½ cup white wine
Grated cheese
Parsley (to garnish)

Brown the onion in oil, add mushrooms and simmer on a low fire. Season scallops, add squeezed garlic. Roll scallops in bread crumbs, and simmer them with the onion for a while. Add wine and grated cheese. Serve, garnished with parsley.

Makes 4 servings

From: **Old Warsaw Cookbook
(France)**

Sole Bonne Femme

Ingredients

½ cup shallots, sliced
½ cup mushrooms, sliced
Pinch chopped parsley
Salt and pepper
2 pounds sole fillets
1 cup dry white wine
1 cup cream

Place the shallots, mushrooms, a sprinkle of the parsley and salt and pepper on the bottom of the pan.* Put the fish on top and pour the wine over. Cover and simmer very gently for 5 minutes or until the fish flakes easily when prodded with a fork. Take out the fish when cooked and place on a platter and keep hot. Add the cream to the pan and boil until reduced by about a quarter. Be very careful not to cook too long, as sauce will burn easily. Pour over the fish and serve with more parsley and tomato slices. Serve with new boiled potatoes and a green salad.

*TIPS:
Use a wide bottomed pan for this dish as it will then be easier to cook the fish without breaking the fillets.

Makes 4 servings

From: *Celtic Cookbook*

Paella a la Valenciana

Ingredients

½ cup olive oil
1 medium chicken, cut into 12 pieces
1 teaspoon paprika
¼ pound diced *chorizo*, or other
    garlic sausage
2 tablespoons diced cured ham
12 raw king prawns or lobster tails
1 large onion, chopped
1 large green pepper, chopped
1 tablespoon chopped parsley
3 cloves garlic, chopped
½ teaspoon crushed saffron
Salt
2 cups long grain rice
1 bay leaf
4 to 5 cups fish stock
3 to 4 squid, cleaned
2 cups mussels or clams, or both, well-scrubbed
1 cup peas, fresh or frozen
2 cups (1 pound) peeled shrimps/prawns
1 canned sweet red pepper
2 lemons, cut into wedges

Put the oil in the *paellera* or large flat pan. Season the chicken pieces and sauté until light golden-brown on both sides—sprinkle with paprika while cooking. Add the diced *chorizo* and ham, and continue cooking for another 5 minutes. Remove the meats from pan with a slotted spoon and set aside.

Add the uncooked lobster tails and/or king prawns in the shells to the pan and cook over high heat for about 3 minutes (turning the pieces occasionally), until the shells begin to turn pink. Then remove from pan and set aside.

In the same pan, cook the chopped onions, peppers, parsley and chopped garlic until soft (add a little more oil if necessary). Stir in saffron and add salt to taste. Now add the rice and mix well with the onion mixture. Add bay leaf, pour in stock and bring to boil. Lower heat immediately, and return the chicken, ham and sausage to the pan and cook the *paella*, uncovered, over low heat for 15 to 20 minutes. After about 10 minutes, add the squid (cut into medium-sized pieces), and a little more water, if necessary.

Meanwhile, put the cleaned mussels and/or clams (use only those with closed shells) in a saucepan of boiling water, add salt to taste. As soon as the shells open, remove from heat. Drain, and discard that half of the shell which does not contain the mussel/clam. Set the mussels/clams aside.

Now add the peas to the *paella* and continue cooking for about 8 to 10 minutes. If necessary, add a little of the strained mussel/clam water. Finally, add the peeled shrimps, together with the previously cooked shellfish: lobster tails, king prawns, mussels, clams, and cook for further 5 minutes or so, until all the liquid has been absorbed and the rice is cooked but not too soft. Remove from heat, cover and allow to stand for 5 minutes. Before serving, decorate the *paella* with strips of the canned sweet red pepper and lemon wedges.

Makes 6 servings

From: *A Spanish Family Cookbook*

Fried Pickled Fish
Pescado en Escabeche

Ingredients

6 fillets of red snapper, pompano, or sole
3 tablespoons lime or lemon juice
½ cup sifted all-purpose flour
3 teaspoons salt, divided
1 teaspoon freshly ground black pepper, divided
1½ cups olive or salad oil, divided
2 cups cider vinegar
½ cup water
1 tablespoon sugar
2 cups thinly sliced onions
2 cups julienne-cut red or green peppers
3 tablespoons capers
2 tablespoons mustard pickles

Cut the fillets in half crosswise and rub with the lime juice; let stand for 10 minutes. Mix together the flour, 2 teaspoons salt, and ¾ teaspoon pepper. Coat the fillets with the mixture. Heat ½ cup oil in a skillet; fry the fish in it until browned on both sides.

In a saucepan, combine the vinegar, water, sugar, onions, peppers, and the remaining salt, pepper, and oil. Bring to a boil and cook over low heat for 5 minutes. Mix in the capers and pickles; pour over the fish and marinate at least 24 hours before serving. Garnish with black olives and cubes of cream cheese, if desired.

Serves 6 as a main course
Serves 12 as an appetizer

From: **The Art of South American Cookery**
(Chile)

201

Marinated Fish, Peruvian Style
Seviche Peruano

Ingredients

2 pounds fillet of red snapper, pompano, or sole
½ cup lime or lemon juice
½ cup peeled, chopped tomatoes
½ cup finely chopped green peppers
1 pimiento, chopped fine
¾ cup finely chopped onions
1 clove garlic, minced
1 tablespoon minced parsley
1 teaspoon salt
⅛ teaspoon dried ground chili peppers
1 teaspoon sugar
¼ cup cider vinegar

Use very fresh fish (frozen fish cannot be substituted). Cut the fillets in finger-length strips; pour the lime or lemon juice over it and turn fish to coat completely. Place in the refrigerator for at least 8 hours. Drain well.

Mix together the tomatoes, green peppers, pimiento, onions, garlic, parsley, salt, chili peppers, sugar, and vinegar. Spread over the fish.

Makes 6 to 8 servings

**From: *The Art of South American Cookery*
(Peru)**

202

Desserts

 **Date Cake**

Ingredients

1⅓ cups chopped dates
2 cups finely chopped almonds (or "almond meal")
4 eggs, separated
1 cup sugar

Toss chopped dates with almond meal until dates are well-coated and don't stick together.

In a bowl start beating egg yolks and then slowly add sugar and then almond-date mixture. Beat egg whites until firm peaks form.Gently fold into date mixture. Bake in 2 well-greased 8-inch cake pans or 1 13 × 9-inch pan in a slow oven (275 degrees) until cake shrinks from side of pan, 1 to 1½ hours. Cool in pan 15 minutes, then turn out and cool on racks.

Makes 6 to 8 servings

From: ***Best of Regional African Cooking***
(Morocco)

Nutmeg Sugar Cookies

Ingredients

1¼ cups all-purpose flour
2 teaspoons baking powder
¼ teaspoon salt
1 stick softened butter
¾ teaspoon ground nutmeg
1 cup sugar
1 large egg
Hundreds and thousands (sprinkles)

Sift flour and baking powder, add salt. Set aside. Blend butter, nutmeg and sugar, beat in egg, stir into flour mixture. Chill overnight or for several hours until stiff enough to roll. Using half at a time, roll to ⅛-inch thickness on a floured board, cut out with biscuit cutter. Sprinkle with hundreds and thousands and bake in a 375 degree oven for 11 minutes or until lightly browned around the edges.

Variation:
Decorate cookies, after baking, with a mixture of icing sugar and water, blended to a smooth paste. Coloring may be added.

Makes 8 to 10 servings

**From: *Cooking the Caribbean Way*
(Grenada)**

 **Walnut Cake**

Ingredients

6 tablespoons butter
½ cup castor sugar
2 tablespoons West India treacle
1 egg, lightly beaten
¾ cup all-purpose flour
½ teaspoon baking soda
1 tablespoon chopped walnuts

Cream the butter and sugar and beat in the warmed treacle. Add the egg, a little at a time, alternately with the flour and baking soda sifted together. Blend thoroughly and stir in the nuts. Bake in a well-greased sandwich tin in a 375 degree oven for about 30 minutes.

TIPS:

The cake may be decorated with this coffee butter icing:
3 tablespoons butter
⅔ cupicing sugar
2 teaspoons coffee essence
Hot water

Cream butter and sugar, beat in essence and continue beating, adding a little hot water, to make a smooth paste. Spread on the cake.

Makes 6 servings

From: *Cooking the Caribbean Way*
(Tobago)

 Bananas Celeste

Ingredients

6 bananas, peeled and halved lengthwise
½ stick butter
8 ounces cream cheese
¼ cup brown sugar
½ teaspoon cinnamon
3 tablespoons thick cream or yogurt

Brown halved bananas in butter and arrange 6 pieces in a buttered pie plate. Cream the cream cheese, sugar and cinnamon and spread half the mixture on bananas. Add another layer of bananas, another layer of cheese mixture and pour cream or yogurt over the top. Bake in a moderate oven (375 degrees) for 20 minutes.

Makes 4 to 6 servings

From: *Cooking the Caribbean Way*
(Martinique)

 **Coconut Macaroons**

Ingredients

3 egg whites
2 tablespoons castor sugar
2 heaping tablespoons all-purpose flour
1 cup grated coconut
½ teaspoon baking powder
1 teaspoon vanilla/almond essence

Whip egg whites stiffly. Beat the sugar into them, then add the flour gradually followed by the rest of the ingredients, beating each in turn into the mixture until it stands up in peaks. In a preheated oven (300 degrees), put spoonfuls of the mixture on a greased baking tray, 1 inch apart, and bake until the coconut macaroons are a light golden-brown, about 20 minutes.

Makes 24 macaroons

From: *The Best of Goan Cooking*

Witches Foam
Hexenschaum

Ingredients

3 medium cooking apples
4 egg whites
¾ cup sugar
2 tablespoons apricot jam
1 teaspoon rum or maraschino
1 tablespoon lemon juice

Bake the apples until they are soft, put through a sieve.

Whisk the egg whites, gradually adding the sugar, jam, apple purée, rum and lemon juice. Continue whisking until it is quite stiff. Chill well before serving.

Makes 4 servings

From: *The Best of Austrian Cuisine*

Mozartkugeln

These are delicious sweets which you normally buy at the Confectioner's, and are more of a "Candy".

for the 1ˢᵗ Mixture
1 cup almonds
1 teaspoon white of egg
About 1 cup icing sugar

for the 2ⁿᵈ Mixture
¾ cup walnuts
1 cup icing sugar
1 teaspoon rum
1 white of egg
2 ounces plain chocolate, melted

for the Coating
3 ounces plain chocolate
1 piece of butter (walnut-size)

Skin and oven-dry the almonds and grate them as finely as possible. Now mix into paste with the egg white and the sugar; if desired add a little green food coloring to this. Form into small balls the size of a small marble. Prepare the 2ⁿᵈ Mixture: grate the walnuts, add the sugar, rum, egg white, and chocolate which you have melted in the oven. Form this into a paste also, and shape over the first little ball. This is done by taking enough of the chocolate mixture into the palm of your hand, then put the first ball on top and coat around it, the covering should be about ¼-inch thick all over.For the chocolate coating: melt the chocolate, adding 2 tablespoons of boiling water and the butter, insert the balls one by one, coating them well and take them out carefully with the tips of 2 forks. Put on wire rack overnight to dry, and then put in white paper cups.

Makes 12 to 15 servings

From: *The Best of Austrian Cuisine*

Bavarian Cream

Ingredients

5 leaves gelatin
1 pound raspberries, fresh or frozen
⅔ cup sugar
1 tablespoon lemon juice
1 cup heavy cream
Pistachio nuts
Whipped cream

Soak the gelatin in cold water. Purée the raspberries (if using frozen fruit, unfreeze before use) in a blender. (Save a few berries for decoration.) Mix the raspberry purée with the sugar and lemon juice until the sugar is dissolved. Pour 6 tablespoons of the mixture into a small saucepan, heat it up and dissolve the squeezed gelatin in it Add the gelatin mixture to the cold raspberry mixture. Wait until mixture begins to set. Whip the heavy cream until it holds stiff peaks and fold carefully but thoroughly into the raspberry mixture. Transfer the mixture into a serving bowl or individual serving glasses and refrigerate at least 3 hours. Garnish with whole raspberries, pistachio nuts and dabs of whipped cream. If you wish to unmold the cream, pour it into a mold rinsed with cold water and let it settle, refrigerated, overnight. Unmold and garnish as desired.

Makes 6 servings

From: *Bavarian Cooking*

Honey Mousse

Ingredients

½ cup crushed pineapple (drained)
½ cup orange blossom honey (warmed)
½ cup nut meats, chopped
½ cup diced candied fruit
1 teaspoon vanilla extract
2 egg whites
¼ cup powdered sugar
1 cup heavy cream

Mix pineapple, honey, nut meats, candied fruit and vanilla. Cool. Beat egg whites until stiff and add sugar. Beat cream until stiff. Fold all ingredients together and freeze either in paper mousse cups or in freezing trays.

Makes 4 to 6 servings

From: *Honey Cookbook*

 # Honey Caramels

Ingredients

¾ cup sugar
¼ cup honey
¼ cup brown sugar
2 tablespoons butter
¼ cup milk
½ cup cream
½ teaspoon vanilla

213

Combine all ingredients except vanilla in a saucepan. Cook to 253 degrees. Stir frequently to prevent scorching. Remove from flame. Add vanilla and pour into buttered 8-inch pan. When cold, cut with sharp knife and wrap each piece in wax paper.

Makes 24 caramels

From: *Honey Cookbook*

 ## Plum Dumplings

Ingredients

1 pound fresh prune plums
3 cups all-purpose flour
Pinch of salt
½ packet dry yeast
1 teaspoon sugar
¾ cup warm milk or so, divided
1 egg
8 tablespoons melted butter
1 cup farmer's cheese

Wash and dry the plums, then cut them in half and remove the stones.

Mix together the flour and salt in a large bowl. Make a well in the center and put in the yeast and the sugar. Mix together the yeast, sugar, and a little of the flour. Slowly add ½ cup of the milk that has been warmed on the stove. Put a warm, damp cloth over the bowl and leave for about 20 minutes or until the yeast mixture has risen a little.

Add the remaining ¼ cup of milk into the yeast mixture and begin to mix in the remaining flour. Break the egg into the flour and keep mixing it in until you have a thick paste.

Turn the dough out onto a floured board or table. Knead it very quickly and lightly just enough to have it form a ball, then, using a pin, roll it out quite thin (about ⅛-inch). Cut the dough into squares with 2-inch sides.

Put half a plum in each square, wrap the dough around the plum, and seal the edges by pinching the sides together.

Bring a large pot of water to a rapid boil. Put about a dozen (12) of the plums into the boiling water. Once the dumplings have risen to the surface of the water, boil them for another 5 minutes. Put a sieve next to the pot and transfer the cooked dumplings into it, piercing each of them with a fork to release their steam. Serve with sugar, melted butter, and farmer's cheese.

Makes 4 to 6 servings

From: The Best of Czech Cooking

Apricot Cream
Barackkrém

Ingredients

8 fresh ripe apricots or ½ cup dried apricots
½ tablespoon gelatin
½ cup sugar
2 tablespoons lemon juice
1 cup heavy cream, whipped

Peel the fresh or cook the dried apricots, and press through a strainer. Dissolve the gelatin and sugar in the lemon juice over hot water. Blend with the apricot pulp. Chill in refrigerator until jelling starts, about 45 minutes. Then fold apricot mixture into whipped cream and chill until time to serve. It may be piled into individual serving dishes before second chilling.

Makes 6 servings

From: *The Art of Hungarian Cooking*

Zolobiya

*Of sweet Zolo-biya chain I hung a necklace around
    her neck.
From its delicious loops I made a ring on her ears.*

Here is a confection which is as old as the story of *One
Thousand and One Nights*, for the name is mentioned in
many stories in the book. It is served only at informal home
parties and nightly gatherings during the month of
Ramadan. It is also a favorite present to the poor during
this month.

For making this confection, the Persians have always
used a mineral salt which is gathered and dried on the
shores of the Persian Gulf. It is white and very fluffy and is
called *kafe darya*, meaning sea foam. Bicarbonate of soda
is an appropriate substitute for it.

Ingredients

½ cup plain yogurt
1 pound wheat starch or cornstarch
1 tablespoon good oil
1 teaspoon soda
3½ cups sugar
2 cups hot water
2 tablespoons honey
Shortening or oil (for deep frying)

Gradually combine yogurt and starch, add oil and soda and
stir well, making a smooth dough, thin enough to flow through
a large funnel. Cover and let rise for 1 hour. Meanwhile, combine sugar and water and boil over high heat until the syrup spins

a thread.Stir in honey and boil for 3 minutes longer. Remove from heat and keep warm.

Heat shortening or oil to a depth of 1 inch in a large frying pan. Pour the batter into the hot oil through a large funnel, blocking half the hole with the middle finger and moving the funnel in a circle to form several circles twisted together and as large as 3 inches in diameter. Cook the circles until golden, dip in the warm syrup, and place in a sieve or on a perforated tray placed over a cookie sheet to drain. Cool and store in a tightly covered container.

Makes 6 to 8 servings

From: *The Art of Persian Cooking*

Danish Apple Cake

Ingredients

1 package (6-ounce) zwieback, finely crushed—about 2
    cups crumbs
6 tablespoons melted butter
2 cups tart applesauce
1 cup raspberry jam
1 cup heavy cream
Sugar
Vanilla

Toss zwieback crumbs with melted butter.Spread ½ cup of the crumbs in bottom of glass serving bowl (about 2-quarts size). Top with 1 cup of the applesauce. Make another layer of ½ cup crumbs; top with a layer of the raspberry jam. Make a third layer of ½ cup crumbs, then a layer of the remaining applesauce; top with remaining crumbs. Cover and chill, or serve immediately. At serving time, whip cream with sugar to sweeten and vanilla to flavor. Pile on top of apple cake in puffs. Spoon cake into dessert glasses or bowls to serve.

Makes 8 servings

From: *The Best of Scandinavian Cooking* (Denmark)

 Ukrainian Pudding

Ingredients

1 cup bread crumbs
4 cups milk
4 eggs, separated
1 cup brown sugar
1 grated lemon rind
¼ cup chopped almonds
1 pinch salt
3 tablespoons butter

Soak bread crumbs in milk ½ hour. Beat yolks well with sugar. Add soaked crumbs, lemon rind, almonds, beaten egg whites, and a pinch of salt. Grease molds with butter. Place batter in the molds. Bake in 350 degree oven for 35 minutes or until firm.

Makes 4 servings

From: *The Best of Ukrainian Cuisine*

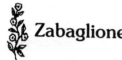

Zabaglione

Ingredients

1 egg yolk per person
1 tablespoon sugar per egg
2 tablespoons marsala or white wine per egg
Dash of lemon rind
Drop of sweet liqueur

Beat the eggs with sugar in a double boiler. When white and fluffy, add wine, and lemon rind. Liqueur is optional. Place on a low flame, mixing constantly with a wooden spoon. Take off the fire at the point of boiling. Serve immediately.

From: *Old Warsaw Cookbook*
(Italy)

Pumpkin Pie

Ingredients

for the Crust
1 teaspoon salt
2 cups all-purpose flour
⅔ cup shortening
Cold water
Mix salt with flour.Cut in shortening with 2 knives or pastry blender until pieces are pea-sized. Sprinkle in cold water

until the material forms a ball. Chill. Divide in half and roll each crust into a circle the size of the pie pan. Sometimes it is easier to handle if rolled between 2 pieces of waxed paper. Place in 2 pans.

for the Filling of 2 pies
2 cups cooked pumpkin
1 teaspoon cinnamon
½ teaspoon ginger
2 eggs, beaten
1 cup brown sugar
½ teaspoon salt
2 cups rich milk

Pumpkin may be either peeled and steamed or baked in shell in a moderate oven. It should be sieved or mashed until smooth for this purpose. Stir together all the ingredients and pour into 2 unbaked pie shells. Bake at 425 degrees for 10 minutes. Reduce heat to 275 degrees and bake 30 minutes longer. In addition to these dishes, the Thanksgiving dinner includes grapefruit, fruit cup or fruit juice for the first course or sometimes a cream soup is served. A tray of relishes, including celery and carrot sticks, is passed. Hot breads or sweet rolls are usually part of the dinner. Hot coffee and mixed nuts bring the feast to a close. After that—bicarbonate of soda!

Makes many servings

From: *Old Warsaw Cookbook*
(America)

221

Milk Pudding Pistachio Nuts

Ingredients

½ cup shelled pistachio nuts
2 heaping tablespoons cornstarch
2 heaping tablespoons rice flour
½ cup cold water
2 quarts milk
1 cup sugar
Dash salt
1 teaspoon vanilla extract

Place whole nuts in a saucepan, cover with water, and boil for 5 minutes. Remove from heat, pour 2 cups of cold water over them, and remove the dark skins of the nuts. Dry in a towel and grind with nut grinder. Set aside.

Place cornstarch and rice flour in a bowl, add ½ cup cold water, stir and set aside.

Place milk in a saucepan, add sugar and salt, and bring to a boil over medium heat. Slowly pour in the cornstarch and rice flour mixture, stirring constantly. Cook about 35 minutes, stirring constantly, until mixture is the consistency of a thick pudding. Add half of the pistachios and the vanilla; mix well. Remove from heat, pour into bowls for individual helpings or into 1 large bowl. Decorate top with the remaining half of the pistachio nuts.

Cool for 2 or 3 hours.

This pudding may be prepared a day in advance and kept in the refrigerator. Serve with lemon cookies.

Makes 6 to 8 servings

From: *The Art of Turkish Cooking*

 **Swedish Pancakes**
Plättar

Ingredients

2 eggs, separated
2 heaping tablespoons all-purpose flour
2 cups rich milk or more
1 tablespoon sugar
Pinch of salt
3 tablespoons melted butter

Beat well the 2 egg yolks. Add alternately flour and milk. Stir in sugar, salt, and melted butter. Make batter preferably a few hours before required. Fold in stiffly beaten egg whites. When butter is used in batter, very little is required for frying.

Makes 4 servings

From: ***The Best of Smorgasbord Cooking (Sweden)***

Swedish Rice Pudding

Ingredients

⅔ cup rice
3 tablespoons butter
2 to 3 tablespoons sugar
½ teaspoon salt
8 bitter almonds, blanched and grated
⅓ cup seedless raisins, scalded
2 to 3 egg yolks

for the Baking dish
½ tablespoon butter
2 tablespoons breadcrumbs

Rinse rice in cold water, put in boiling slightly salted water and boil briskly for 15 minutes. Draw and rinse under cold water and drain. Put into saucepan, divide butter into small portions and stir into rice with a fork. Cover saucepan and leave in hot oven (400 degrees) for about 15 minutes, stirring often with a fork. Pour into mixing bowl and mix with cold butter, salt, sugar, blanched and grated almonds, and well-rinsed and -scalded seedless raisins. When cold, stir in well-beaten yolks. Pour into buttered and breadcrumbed baking-dish, and bake in moderate oven (385 degrees) for 40 to 50 minutes. Serve only just warm, with jam, compôte or fruit syrup sauce.

Makes 6 servings

From: *Good Food from Sweden*

London Buns

Ingredients

7½ cups all-purpose
    flour
½ cup castor sugar
2 tablespoons
    yeast
¾ stick butter
2 cups warm milk
2 tablespoons candied orange peel (cut small)

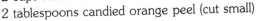

Sift the flour and sugar into a basin and test the yeast with a little of the sugar—about a large teaspoonful. Melt the butter in a saucepan, add the milk, and heat gently until lukewarm. Pour the warm milk and melted butter into the centre of the flour and mix all together with the peel into a dough. Let it rise in a warm place for about 2 hours. Knead and form into round buns; this quantity should make 24. Place them on a greased baking sheet and let them prove. Bake in a 400-degree oven, and directly they come from the oven brush them over with equal quantities of egg and sugar mixed, to glaze them.

Makes 24 servings

From: *Traditional Food from England*

225

Manx Pudding

Ingredients

Pinch of salt
¼ cup plain flour
2 eggs
1 cup milk
⅛ cup currants

Mix salt and flour. Make a well in the center and add the eggs and milk. Add currants and place in a basin to steam for about 2 hours.

Makes 2 servings

From: *Celtic Cookbook*

Baklava
Baklavas

Ingredients

5 cups coarsely chopped walnuts
½ cup sugar
¼ cup plain dried bread crumbs
1 tablespoon ground cinnamon
1 tablespoon ground cloves
1 cup unsalted butter, melted (divided)
1 teaspoon vanilla
1 pound fillo dough

Preheat oven to 325 degrees. In a large bowl, mix the walnuts, sugar, bread crumbs, cinnamon and cloves. Add ¼ cup of the melted butter and the vanilla. Mix together carefully.

Brush butter on all the sides and bottom of a 18 × 12 × 3-inch jelly roll pan. Layer 5 sheets of fillo dough in the pan, brushing each layer with butter. Evenly spread 1½ cups of the walnut mixture over the top layer. Fold in the long sides of the fillo, and brush them with melted butter. Add 3 more fillo sheets, brushing each one with butter. Add 3 more fillo sheets, brushing with butter, and top with remaining walnut mixture. Turn the sides in and continue adding remaining fillo sheets, brushing each with butter. With a sharp knife, cut diagonally across the top to mark into diamond shaped pieces. Brush the top with butter very thoroughly until all sides and top are completely covered. Sprinkle with water and bake for 1 hour, or until golden-brown.

for the Syrup
3 cups sugar
4 cups water
½ cup honey
1 stick cinnamon
3 whole cloves
2 tablespoons lemon juice
1 slice lemon peel

Mix together all ingredients and boil for 15 minutes. Remove the cinnamon, cloves and lemon peel. Cool completely. Spoon the cold syrup over the hot baklava.

Let the baklava stand at room temperature for 6 hours before serving.

Makes 3 dozen

From: *Best of Greek Cuisine: Cooking With Georgia*

Flan
Caramel Custard

Ingredients

for the **Caramel**
5 tablespoons sugar

Put the 5 tablespoons sugar in a small saucepan over a moderate heat and allow to melt. When it starts to change color, stir gently until the syrup becomes a deep golden-brown. Pour the caramel into 6 small molds or 1 soufflé dish, moving the dish/molds quickly to coat the bottom and sides with the caramel.

for the **Custard**
3 large whole eggs (or 4 medium)
3 egg yolks
2 to 3 tablespoons sugar
½ to 1 teaspoon vanilla extract/essence
3 cups milk

Put the eggs, egg yolks, sugar and vanilla extract into a large bowl and whisk. Heat the milk to boiling point, allow to cool for 1 minute or so, then pour the hot milk onto the egg mixture gradually.

Stir well, then pour the custard into the dish/molds. Stand in a bain-marie or roasting pan containing hot water, cover with wax paper and bake in a preheated, moderate oven until the custard is set (about 40 minutes).

When set, remove from the oven and wait until the custard is cold before turning out onto a serving dish.

Makes 6 servings

From: *A Spanish Family Cookbook*

Venezuelan Cheesecake
Torta Criolla de Queso

Ingredients

8 egg yolks
1 cup sugar
1 pound cream cheese
1 teaspoon baking powder
8 egg whites, stiffly beaten

Preheat oven to 375 degrees. Beat the egg yolks and sugar until thick and light. Have the cheese at room temperature and beat in. Stir in the baking powder; then fold in the egg whites thoroughly. Turn into a buttered, 8-inch spring-form pan. Bake for 45 minutes, or until a cake tester comes out clean. Cool.

Makes 8 to 12 servings

From: *The Art of South American Cookery*
(Venezuela)

Brazil-Nut Cake
Torta de Castaanha do Pará

Ingredients

10 egg yolks
1 teaspoon instant coffee
1¾ cups superfine sugar
3 cups ground Brazil nuts
⅛ teaspoon salt
2 tablespoons cognac
2 tablespoons bread crumbs
10 egg whites
1½ cups heavy cream
2 tablespoons coffee essence
3 tablespoons confectioners' sugar
¼ cup slivered Brazil nuts

Preheat oven to 350 degrees. Butter a 10-inch spring-form pan and dust lightly with bread crumbs.

Beat the egg yolks and instant coffee; gradually add the sugar, beating until thick and light. Mix in the ground nuts, salt, cognac, and the 2 tablespoons bread crumbs. Beat the egg whites until stiff but not dry; fold into the nut mixture. Turn into the prepared pan. Bake for 50 minutes, or until a cake tester comes out clean. Cool on a cake rack before removing the pan.

Whip the cream; fold in the coffee essence and confectioners' sugar (if you don't have bottled coffee essence, dissolve 1 tablespoon instant coffee in 2 tablespoons water). Split the cake and spread cream between the layers and over the top and sides. Decorate with the slivered nuts.

Makes 8 to 12 servings

From: The Art of South American Cookery
(Brazil)

Drinks & Cocktails

Wedding Rum Punch

Ingredients

Scant 1 cup Grenadine
Scant 2 cups lemon juice
2¾ cups falernum (see recipe below)
2¾ cups Barbados rum
2¾ ounces Demerara rum
4¾ cups unsweetened pineapple juice, canned
10 dashes Angostura bitters
Ice
Orange slices
Cucumber, sliced thinly

Stir all ingredients together—Grenadine, lemon juice, falernum, Barbados rum, Demerara rum, pineapple, Angostura—in a large punch bowl with plenty of ice.* Float thin slices of orange and cucumber on top to garnish.

*TIPS:

To make a bubbly punch, use less ice and, just before serving, add plenty of well-chilled ginger ale.

Makes 25 servings

**From: *Cooking the Caribbean Way*
        (Bermuda)**

 # Velvet Hammer

Ingredients

½ teaspoon sugar or lime
1 tablespoon lemon or lime juice
½ tablespoon falernum*
1 teaspoon grenadine
1 tablespoon fresh pineapple juice
1 tablespoon dry sherry
1 tablespoon Barbados rum
1 tablespoon Demerara rum
½ tablespoon Jamaica rum
Crushed ice

Shake all ingredients well together. Strain into whiskey sour glasses.

*TIPS:
Falernum is a sugar syrup with an almond essence made from the same sugar cane as rum.

Makes 1 serving

From: *Cooking the Caribbean Way*
(Bermuda)

233

Spiced Tea

Ingredients

3 or 4 blades mace according to strength desired
1 cup water
Sugar
Nutmeg, grated

Boil mace in water for 15 minutes. Strain, add sugar to taste to liquid, and serve with sprinkling of nutmeg.

Serve very hot as a warming drink to give relief from colds, influenza etc.

Variations
Rum, milk or cream can be added.

Makes 1 serving

From: **Cooking the Caribbean Way**
       (Grenada)

Mixed Fruit Cordial

Ingredients

6 tablespoons sugar
6 tablespoons water
Juice of 4 large oranges
Juice of 2 lemons
Juice of 2 grapefruit
Syrup
Iced water or iced soda water
Lemon or lime slices

Boil sugar and water for 2 minutes, then allow to cool. Strain fruit juices and chill for at least 2 hours. Sweeten to taste with syrup and dilute with plain or soda water. Serve in glasses with frosted rims and decorate with lemon or lime slices.

Makes 4 to 6 servings

From: *Cooking the Caribbean Way*
(Trinidad)

 **Ginger Wine**

Ingredients

1 pound raisins
2 ounces ginger, well-bruised
1 gallon water
2½ pounds Demerara sugar
3 limes or 2 lemons, peeled and thinly sliced

Add raisins and ginger to water and bring to a boil. Boil for 30 minutes. Pour in sugar and lemons and stir. Cool, strain into a jar and cover.

It will be ready for use in 1 week.

Makes many servings

From: *Cooking the Caribbean Way*
(British Guiana)

Bluebeard's Rum Custard Pudding

Ingredients

5 eggs
2 tablespoons brown sugar
1 tablespoon corn flour
1½ cups milk
2 tablespoons rum

Beat eggs well, stir in sugar and corn flour. Bring milk to a boil and, stirring all the time, slowly pour in egg mixture. Continue cooking over a very gentle heat, stirring constantly until custard thickens. Remove from heat, stir in rum and pour into individual glasses. Chill and serve very cold.

Makes 4 to 6 servings

From: *Cooking the Caribbean Way*
     (U. S. Virgin Islands)

 Cranberry Cider

Ingredients

2 pounds cranberries
1 gallon boiling water
2½ cups sugar
1 ounce yeast

Wash the berries. Place in a pot with cold water to cover. Boil until the berries pop. Strain into a crock, pour on boiling water, and add sugar. When lukewarm, add yeast dissolved in a little water. Cover, and place in a warm spot.

The next day, skim the top. Pour into bottles and cork. Keep in a cool place. The cider is ready to drink in 2 to 3 days.

Makes 4 quart bottles of ciders

From: *Lithuanian Cookbook*

 ## George IV's Rum Drink c. 1825

Ingredients

Peel of 2 Seville oranges
Peel of 12 lemons
8 cups rum
8 cups cold spring water
2½ cups loaf sugar
2 cups strong green tea
½ cup maraschino
2 cups lemon juice
2 cups Madeira
1 grated nutmeg
2 cups boiling milk

Infuse the peels of the oranges and lemons in the rum for 12 hours. Add water, loaf sugar, green tea, maraschino, lemon juice, Madeira and nutmeg. Mix all together and stir in boiling milk last. Let stand for 6 hours, then strain through a jelly bag until quite clear, and bottle for use.

Makes many servings

From: *English Royal Cookbook: Favorite Court Recipes*

Raspberry Cordial
malinówka

Ingredients

½ jar raspberries, hulled, washed and drained*
Spirits

Fill large jar ½ full with hulled, washed, drained raspberries. Fill jar nearly to top with spirits, seal, let stand at room temperature for 4 to 6 weeks. Strain liquid through cotton-filled funnel into bottles, seal, and set aside. Cover leftover fruit in jar with sugar , using 1 part sugar to 2 parts fruit by weight. (Fruit should be weighed at beginning before being drenched with spirits.) Seal and let stand another 4 to 6 weeks, shaking occasionally. Strain into bottles through cotton-filled funnel, seal, and let stand several days. Combine with first mixture and strain again into bottles, seal, and allow to age several weeks or months.

*TIPS:
Instead of raspberries, you may use blueberries, blackberries, lingonberries, wild strawberries, and other berries.

Makes many servings

From: Polish Heritage Cookery

Coffee Cocktail
Coquetel de Café

Ingredients

1 egg yolk
1 tablespoon sugar
1 cup strong coffee
1 cup port wine
½ cup brandy
1 cup cream
½ cup crushed ice

Beat egg yolk well. Add and beat in the sugar, coffee, port wine, brandy, cream, and shake with crushed ice.

Makes 6 servings

From: *The Art of Brazilian Cookery*

239

Coffee Mazagran
Cafea Mazagran

This is a cool, refreshing drink, enjoyed during hot summer evenings at garden and terrace coffee houses. It was named after General Mazagran who apparently first concocted it during the Crimean War in the 1850s.*

Ingredients

8 cups French Roast coffee
2 tablespoons chicory
Sugar
¼ cup rum
Whipped cream

Brew a pot of coffee using the French Roast coffee mixed with the chicory. Let cool and place in a bottle in the refrigerator.

When ready to serve, pour cold, black coffee into tall glasses filled with crushed ice. Add sugar to taste, and a bit of rum into each glass. Stir well, and spoon whipped cream on top. Serve with a straw.

*TIPS:
Prepare coffee ahead of time or the day before serving.

Makes 8 servings

From: *Taste of Romania*

Chocolate Liqueur
Likier Czekoladowy

Ingredients

6 egg yolks
1 cup sugar
3 ounces baking chocolate
4 tablespoons light cream
2 cups vodka
½ cup whipping cream

Combine yolks and sugar. Whip until frothy. Heat the chocolate and light cream in the top of a double boiler until melted, then combine with the egg mixture and the vodka. Pour into glasses and top with the whipped cream.

Makes 6 servings

From: *The Best of Polish Cooking*

Burnt Punch for New Year's Eve

Ingredients

1 cup chopped figs
1 cup chopped dates
1 cup chopped candied fruit peel
About 2½ cups lump sugar
2 tablespoons grated orange rind
1 cup brandy or rum
4 cups wine
2 sticks cinnamon
Strips of lemon peel
2 cups hot tea
Juice of 2 lemons
Juice of 2 oranges

As midnight approaches, place a deep earthenware or glass baking dish in the center of the table. Into it put the figs, dates, and fruit peel. Place a meshed grill over the fruit and pile sugar on it. Sprinkle with the orange rind, then with the brandy or rum. Let stand until all is absorbed by the sugar.

Put out the lights and, with a taper, light the brandy. While it burns, boil together on the stove the wine, cinnamon, and lemon peel. When the enchanting blue flame of the brandy has burned itself out, pour over the fruits the hot wine, tea, and fruit juices. Stir, and serve in punch glasses with some of the fruit in each one.

Makes 25 to 30 servings

From: *The Art of Hungarian Cooking*

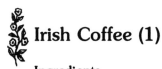

Irish Coffee (1)

Ingredients

1½ teaspoons sugar
Hot, strong black coffee
1 jigger Irish whiskey
1 tablespoon whipped cream

Heat a steamed whiskey goblet. Add the sugar and enough of the hot coffee to dissolve the sugar. Stir well. Add the Irish whiskey and fill the glass to within an inch of the brim with more very hot black coffee. Float the cream on top. Do not mix the cream through the coffee. The hot, whiskey-laced coffee is sipped through the velvety cream.

Irish Coffee (2)

Ingredients

1 teaspoon sugar
Hot, strong black coffee
1 jigger Irish whiskey
1 tablespoon double cream

Proceed as for *Irish Coffee (1)* until the goblet is filled with the spirituous coffee to within an inch of the brim. Gently pour the double cream onto a teaspoon that is held over the coffee. The cream spilling over should float on top of the coffee. But this won't work unless the cream is rich and chilled.

For both recipes: makes 1 serving

From: *The Art of Irish Cooking*

 **Milk of the Wild Cow Cocktail**

Fill the shaker half full of broken ice and add:

Ingredients

⅔ part: Dry Gin
⅓ part: Grenadine
1 teaspoon of fresh cream

Shake well and strain into a cocktail glass.

Makes 1 serving

From: ***The Best of Smorgasbord Cooking***
(Sweden)

Mother-In-Law Tea

Ingredients

3 oranges, untreated
1 lemon, untreated
About ½ cup sugar cubes
Juice of 5 oranges
4 cups water
5 tablespoons tea leaves
4 tablespoons rum

Wash the oranges and the lemon well and rub down the skins with the sugar cubes. Put the orange sugar into a bowl and add the juice of 5 oranges and of the lemon. Stir, cover and let draw for at least 1 hour. Pour the boiling water over the tea leaves, let draw briefly and strain. Mix the tea with the orange juice mixture and the rum and heat it up again. Do not let it boil! Pour into a teapot and serve with Christmas cookies. If there are children in the company, serve the rum separately.

Makes 6 servings

From: *Bavarian Cooking*

Hippocrene is NUMBER ONE in
International Cookbooks

Africa and Oceania
Best of Regional African Cooking
Egyptian Cooking
Good Food from Australia
Traditional South African Cookery

Asia and Near East
Best of Goan Cooking
Best of Kashmiri Cooking
The Joy of Chinese Cooking
The Art of South Indian Cooking
The Art of Persian Cooking
The Art of Israeli Cooking
The Art of Turkish Cooking
The Art of Uzbek Cooking

Mediterranean
Best of Greek Cuisine
Taste of Malta
A Spanish Family Cookbook

Western Europe
Art of Dutch Cooking
Best of Austrian Cuisine
A Belgian Cookbook
Celtic Cookbook
English Royal Cookbook
The Swiss Cookbook
Traditional Recipes from Old
  England
The Art of Irish Cooking
Traditional Food from Scotland
Traditional Food from Wales

Scandinavia
Best of Scandinavian Cooking
The Best of Finnish Cooking
The Best of Smorgasbord
  Cooking
Good Food from Sweden

Central Europe
Best of Albanian Cooking
All Along the Danube
Bavarian Cooking
Traditional Bulgarian Cooking
The Best of Czech Cooking
The Art of Hungarian Cooking
Lithuanian Cooking
Polish Heritage Cookery
The Best of Polish Cooking
Old Warsaw Cookbook
Old Polish Traditions
Taste of Romania

Eastern Europe
The Cuisine of Armenia
The Best of Russian Cooking
The Best of Ukrainian Cuisine

Americas
Cooking the Caribbean Way
Mayan Cooking
The Honey Cookbook
The Art of Brazilian Cookery
The Art of South American
  Cookery